ESSENTIAL
Skills and Practice
Your all-in-one source for school success!

Thinking Kids™
An imprint of Carson-Dellosa Publishing LLC
Greensboro, North Carolina

Thinking Kids™
An imprint of Carson-Dellosa Publishing, LLC
P.O. Box 35665
Greensboro, NC 27425 USA

ISBN 978-1-4838-0242-8

04-334157784

Table of Contents

Essential Skills and Practice Grade PK

Letter *Aa*

A a

Color the alligator and the apple.

Print the uppercase "A."

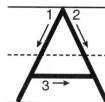

Print the lowercase "a."

Letter A*a*

Color the uppercase letters red.
Color the lowercase letters blue.

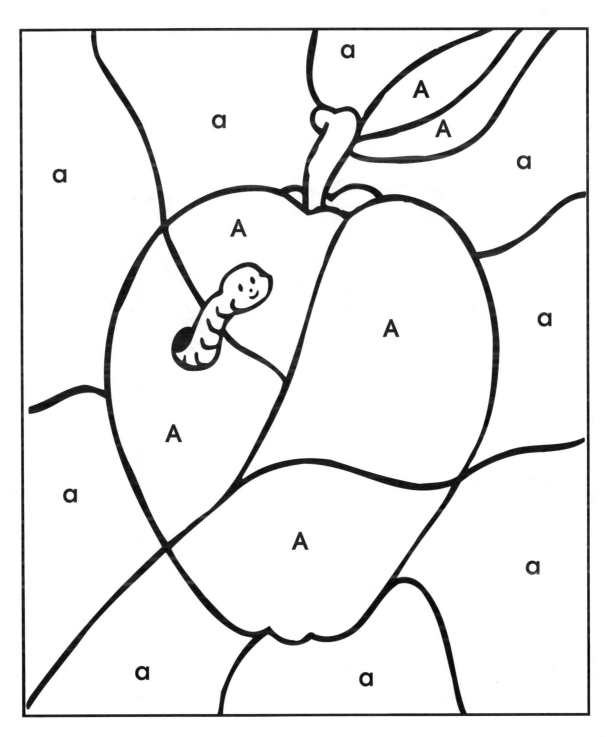

Essential Skills and Practice Grade PK

Letter *Bb*

Bb

Color the bird, balloon, and butterfly.

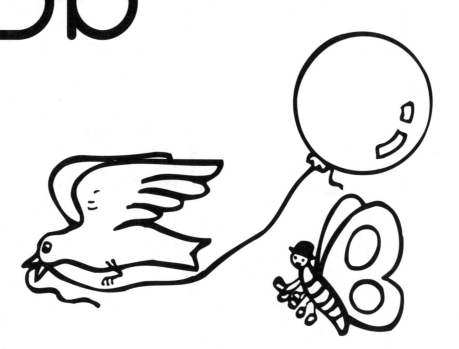

Print the uppercase "B."

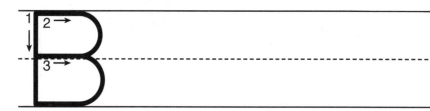

Print the lowercase "b."

Letter *Bb*

Color the uppercase letters red.
Color the lowercase letters blue.

Essential Skills and Practice Grade PK

Letter Cc

Color the car and the cat.

Print the uppercase "C."

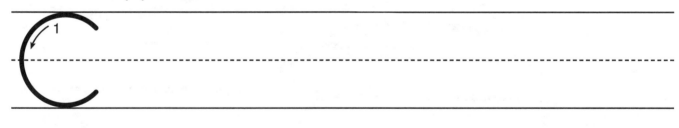

Print the lowercase "c."

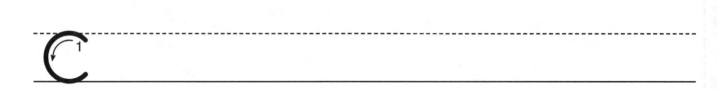

Letter Cc

Color the uppercase letters green.
Color the lowercase letters yellow.

Essential Skills and Practice Grade PK

Letter **Dd**

Dd

Color the dog and the duck.

Print the uppercase "D."

Print the lowercase "d."

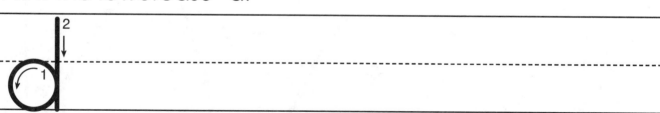

Letter **D**d

Color the uppercase letters gray.
Color the lowercase letters tan.

Essential Skills and Practice Grade PK

Name _____

Letter *Ee*

Ee

Color the elephant and the egg.

Print the uppercase "E."

Print the lowercase "e."

Letter *Ee*

Color the uppercase letters gray.
Color the lowercase letters yellow.

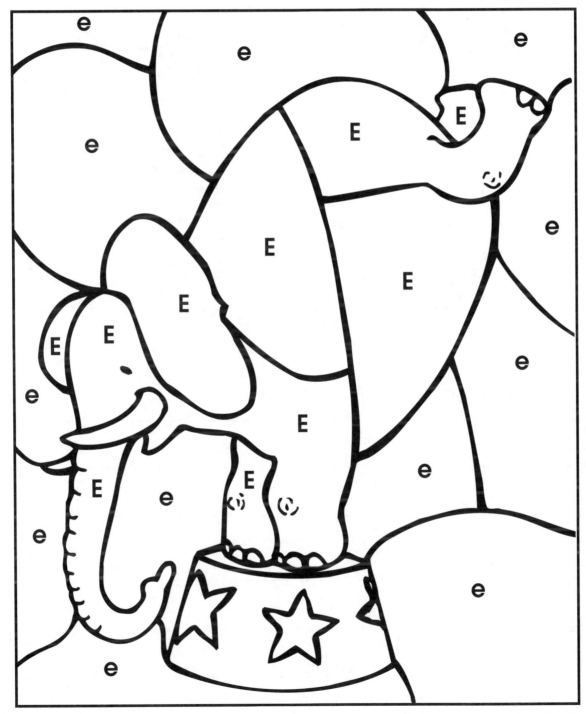

Essential Skills and Practice Grade PK

Letter *Ff*

Color the fox and the fish.

F f

Print the uppercase "F."

Print the lowercase "f."

Letter *Ff*

Color the uppercase letters green.
Color the lowercase letters blue.

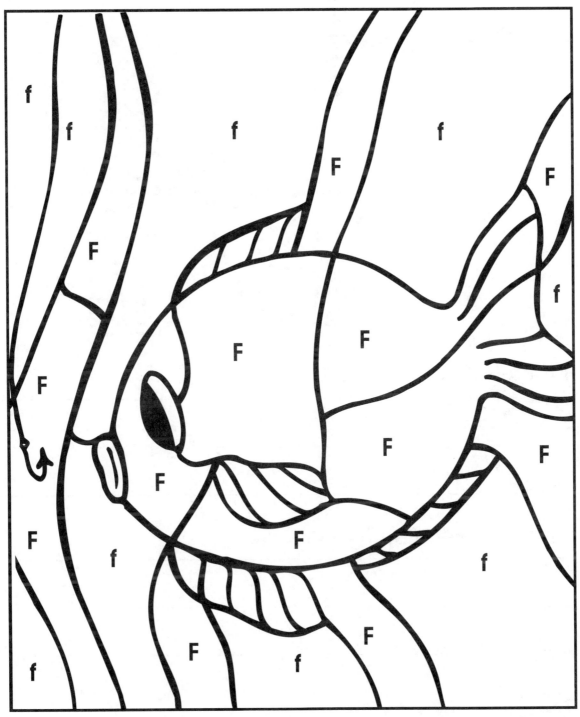

Essential Skills and Practice Grade PK

Name _____

Color the girl and the goat.

Gg

Print the uppercase "G."

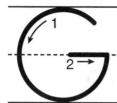

Print the lowercase "g."

Letter Gg

Color the uppercase letters red.
Color the lowercase letters pink.

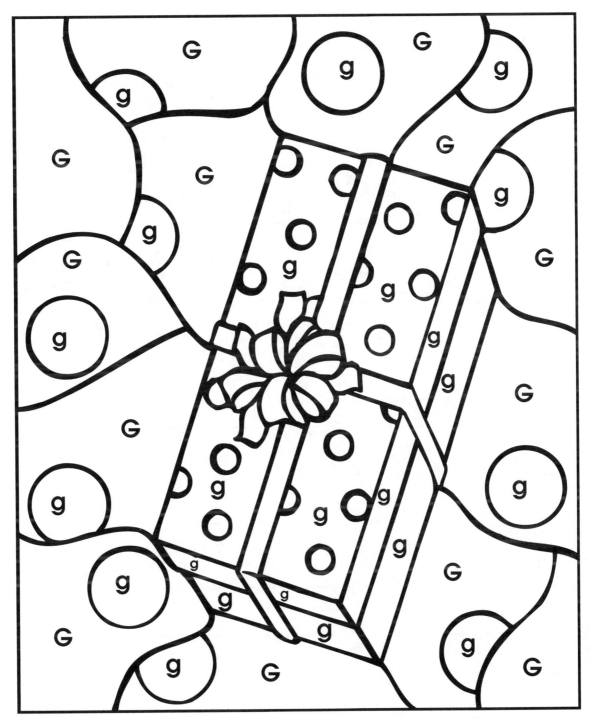

Essential Skills and Practice Grade PK

Name _____

Color the horse and the hat.

Print the uppercase "H."

Print the lowercase "h."

Essential Skills and Practice Grade PK

Letter *Hh*

Color the uppercase letters white.
Color the lowercase letters light blue.

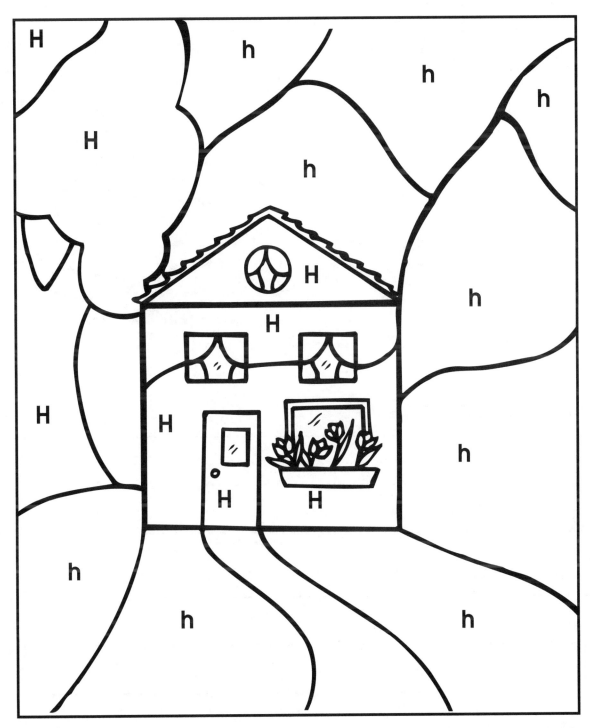

Essential Skills and Practice Grade PK

Letter *Ii*

I i

Color the igloo and the inchworm.

Print the uppercase "I."

Print the lowercase "i."

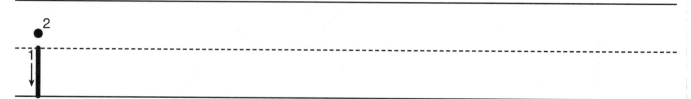

Letter *Ii*

Color the uppercase letters light blue.
Color the lowercase letters dark blue.

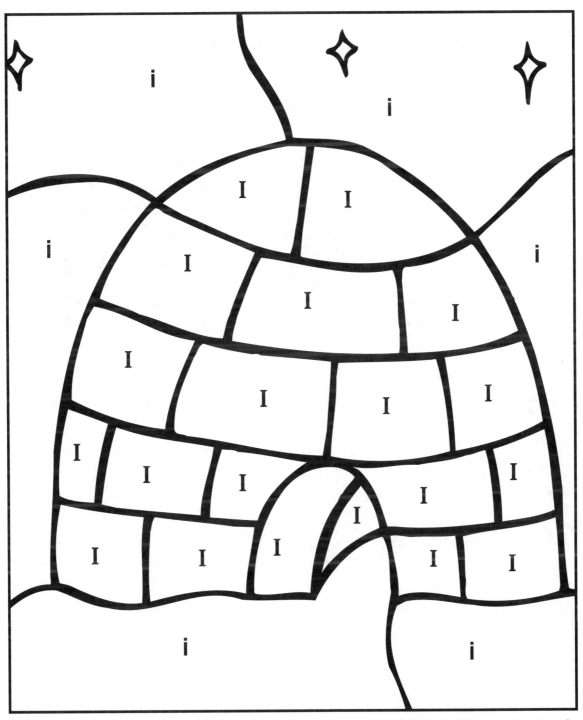

Essential Skills and Practice Grade PK

Name _____

Color the jam and the jack-in-the-box.

Print the uppercase "J."

Print the lowercase "j."

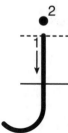

Letter *Jj*

Color the uppercase letters green.
Color the lowercase letters yellow.

Essential Skills and Practice Grade PK

Letter *Kk*

Kk

Color the katydid
and the kangaroo.

Print the uppercase "K."

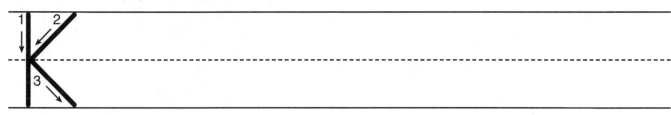

Print the lowercase "k."

Letter *Kk*

Color the uppercase letters gray.
Color the lowercase letters red.

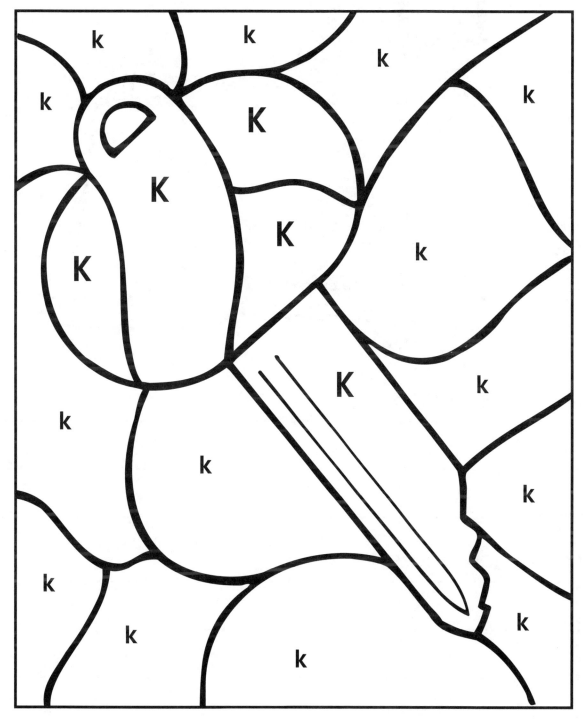

Essential Skills and Practice Grade PK

Letter *Ll*

L l

Color the lion, the lamb, and the lighthouse.

Print the uppercase "L."

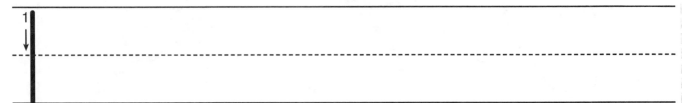

Print the lowercase "l."

Letter *Ll*

Color the uppercase letters purple.
Color the lowercase letters pink.

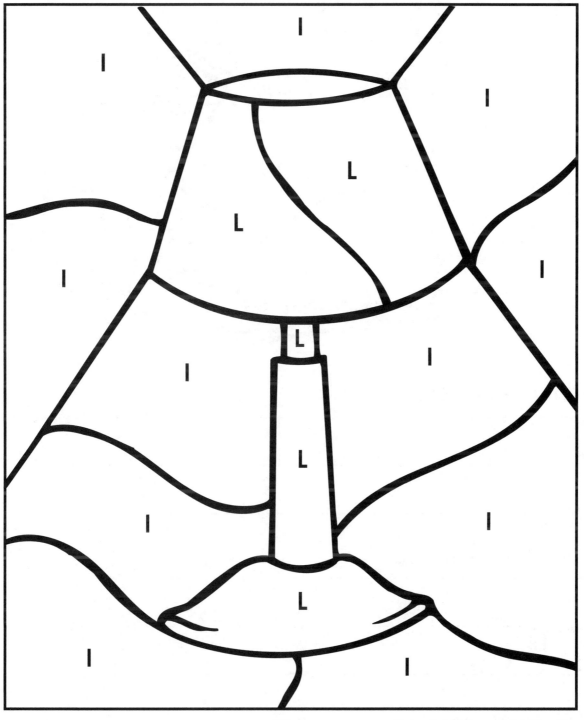

Name _____

Mm

Color the mouse and
the monkey.

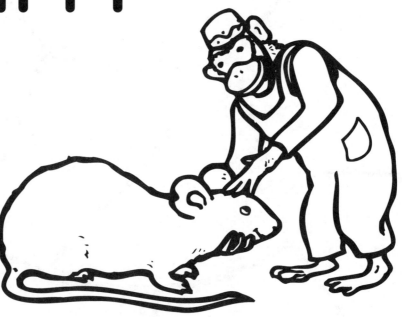

Print the uppercase "M."

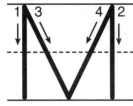

Print the lowercase "m."

Letter *Mm*

Color the uppercase letters yellow.
Color the lowercase letters black.

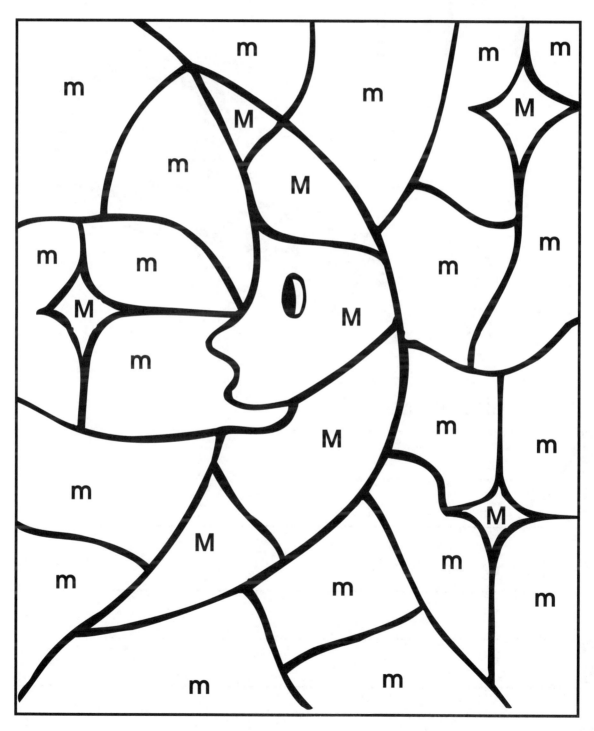

Letter *Nn*

Color the necklace, the nose, and the nest.

Print the uppercase "N."

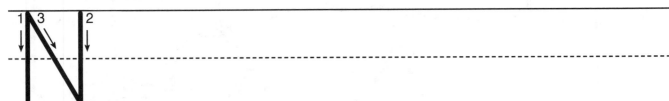

Print the lowercase "n."

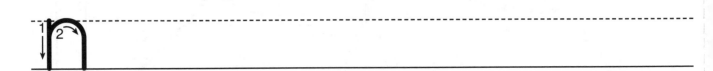

Letter Nn

Color the uppercase letters green.
Color the lowercase letters brown.

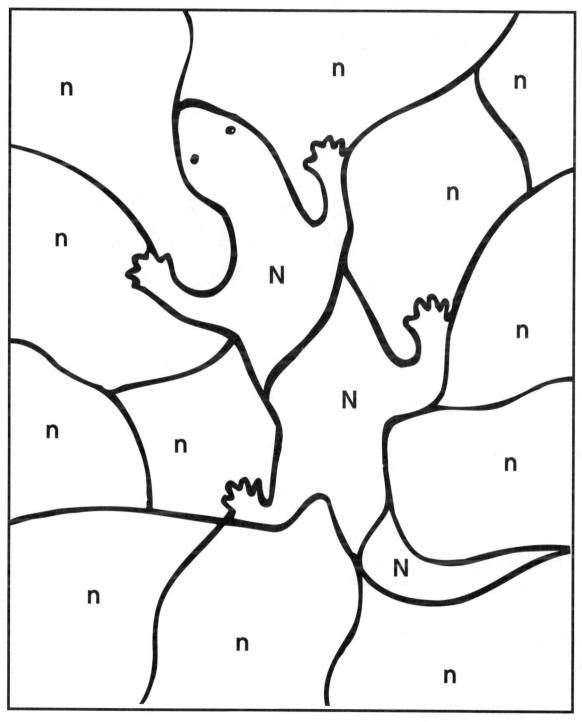

Essential Skills and Practice Grade PK

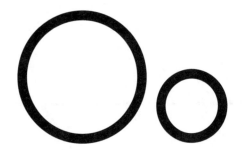

Letter **Oo**

Color the octopus and
the otter.

Print the uppercase "O."

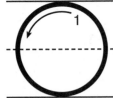

Print the lowercase "o."

Letter *Oo*

Color the uppercase letters brown.
Color the lowercase letters blue.

Essential Skills and Practice Grade PK

Letter *Pp*

P p

Color the penguin and the panda.

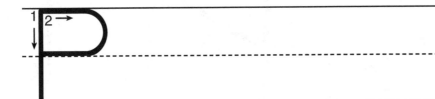

Print the uppercase "P."

P

Print the lowercase "p."

p

Essential Skills and Practice Grade PK

Letter *Pp*

Color the uppercase letters dark green.
Color the lowercase letters light green.

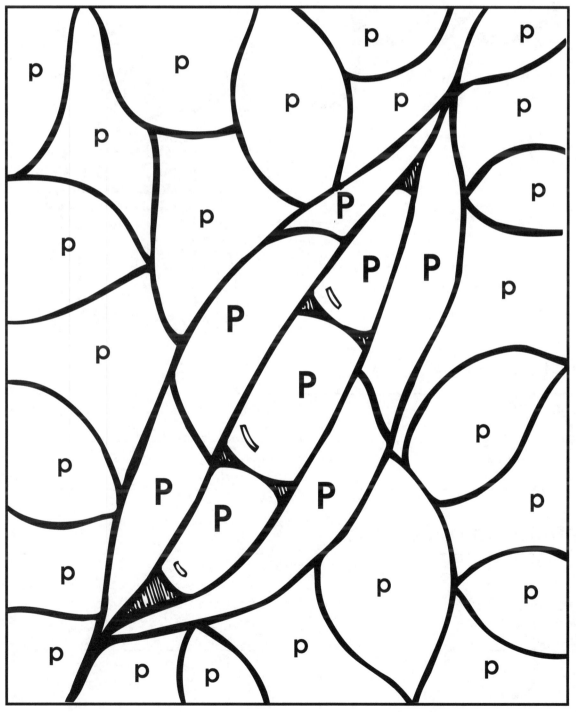

Essential Skills and Practice Grade PK

Letter *Qq*

Qq

Color the queen and her quill pen.

Print the uppercase "Q."

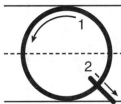

Print the lowercase "q."

Letter *Qq*

Color the uppercase letters purple.
Color the lowercase letters orange.

R r

Letter *Rr*

Color the raccoon and the rabbit.

Print the uppercase "R."

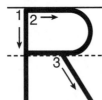

Print the lowercase "r."

Letter *Rr*

Color the uppercase letters red.
Color the lowercase letters green.

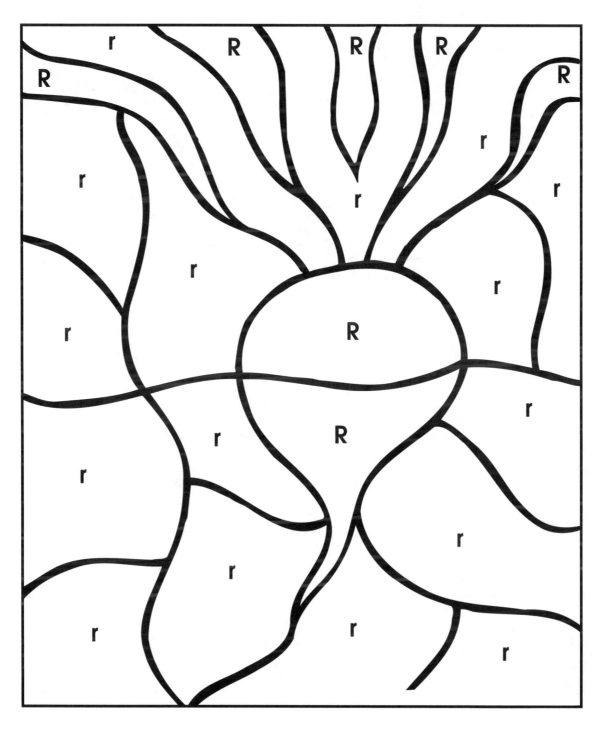

Essential Skills and Practice Grade PK

Name _____

Ss

Color the seal and
the sea horse.

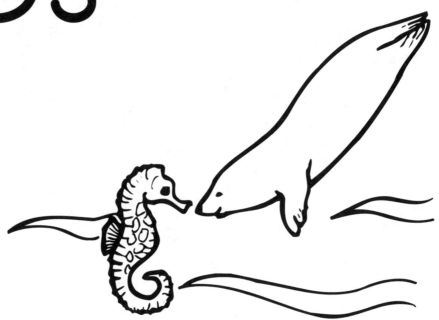

Print the uppercase "S."

Print the lowercase "s."

Letter *Ss*

Color the uppercase letters yellow.
Color the lowercase letters green.

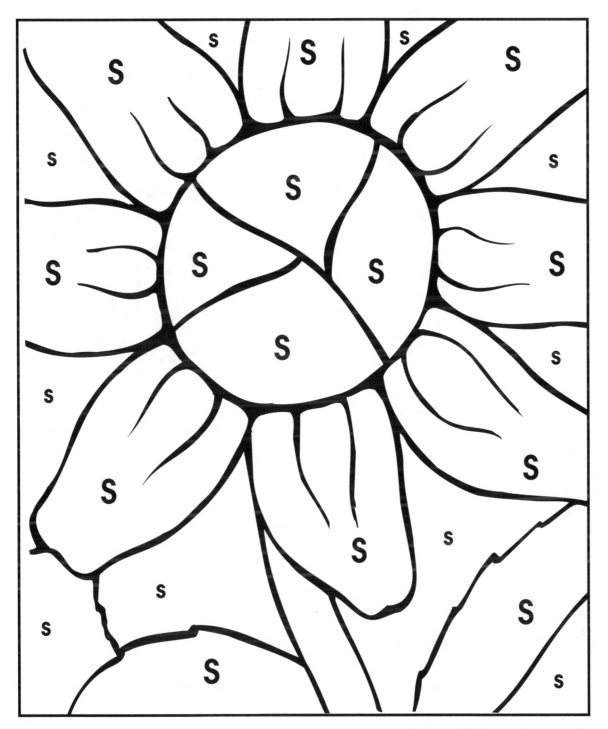

Essential Skills and Practice Grade PK

Letter *Tt*

Color the tapir and
the tiger.

Print the uppercase "T."

Print the lowercase "t."

Letter *Tt*

Color the uppercase letters green.
Color the lowercase letters blue.

Essential Skills and Practice Grade PK

Letter *Uu*

U u

Color the umbrella and the unicorn.

Print the uppercase "U."

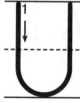

Print the lowercase "u."

Essential Skills and Practice Grade PK

Letter *Uu*

Color the uppercase letters purple.
Color the lowercase letters blue.

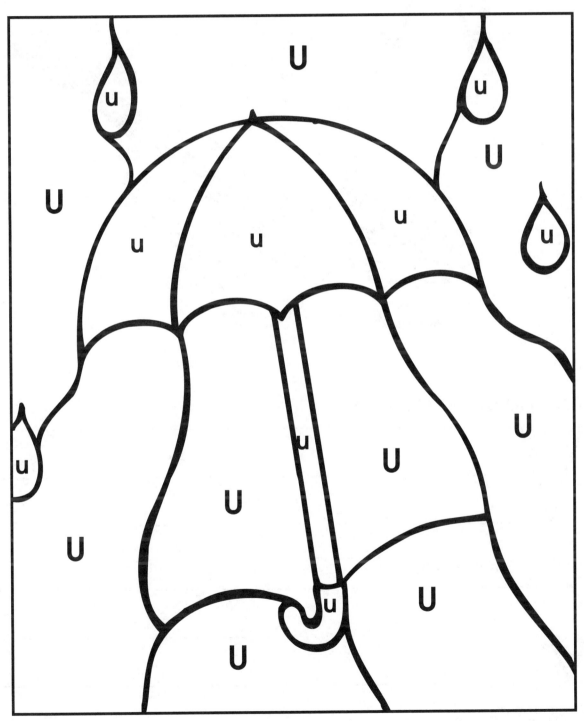

Essential Skills and Practice Grade PK

Letter *Vv*

V v

Color the violets and
the violin.

Print the uppercase "V."

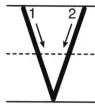

Print the lowercase "v."

Letter *Vv*

Color the uppercase letters orange.
Color the lowercase letters green.

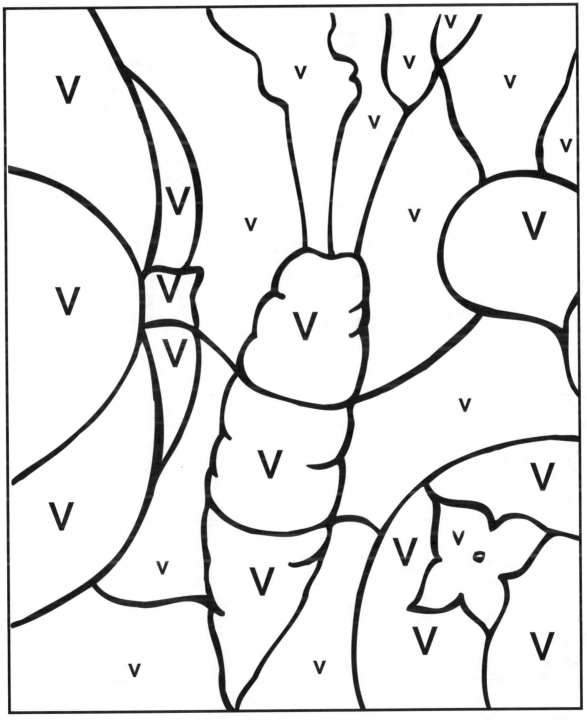

Essential Skills and Practice Grade PK

Letter *Ww*

Color the wolf and
the wombat.

Print the uppercase "W."

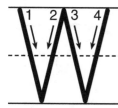

Print the lowercase "w."

Letter *Ww*

Color the uppercase letters black.
Color the lowercase letters gray.

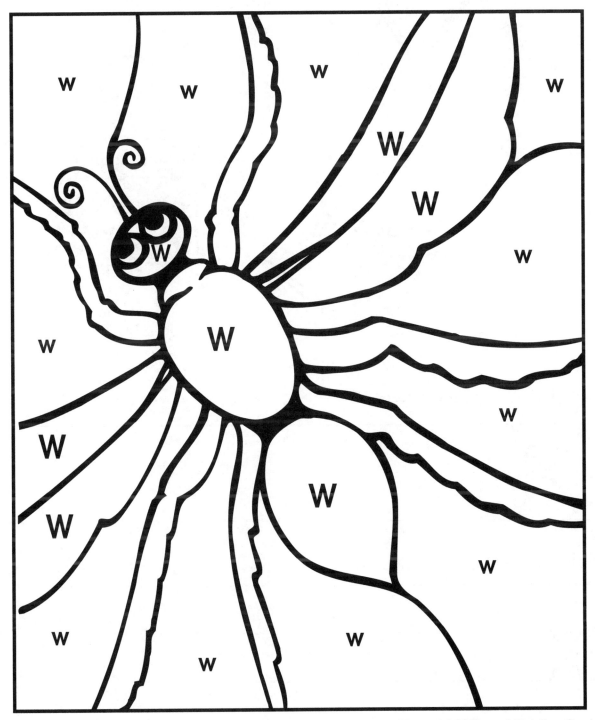

Essential Skills and Practice Grade PK

Letter Xx

Color the xylophone and the X-ray.

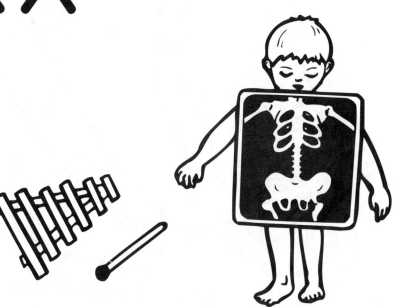

Print the uppercase "X."

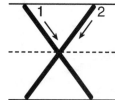

Print the lowercase "x."

Essential Skills and Practice Grade PK

Letter Xx

Color the uppercase letters gold.
Color the lowercase letters blue.

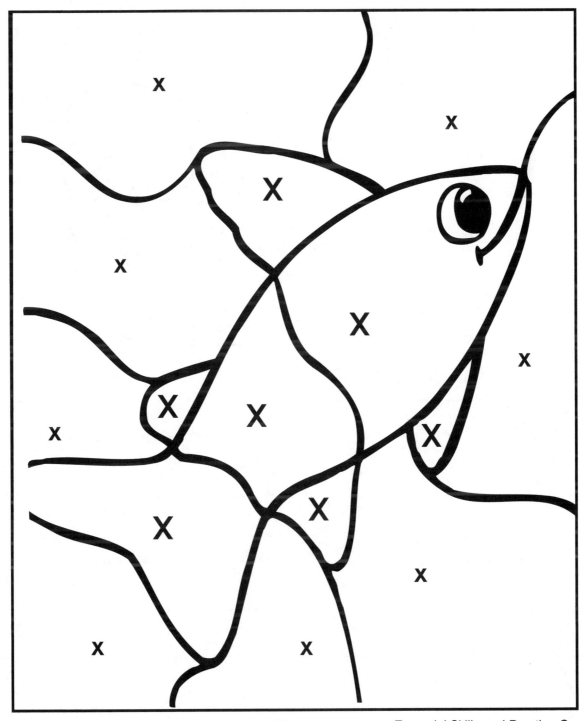

Name _____

Letter *Yy*

Color the yak and the yams.

Print the uppercase "Y."

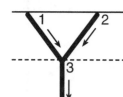

Print the lowercase "y."

Essential Skills and Practice Grade PK

Letter *Yy*

Color the uppercase letters red.
Color the lowercase letters purple.

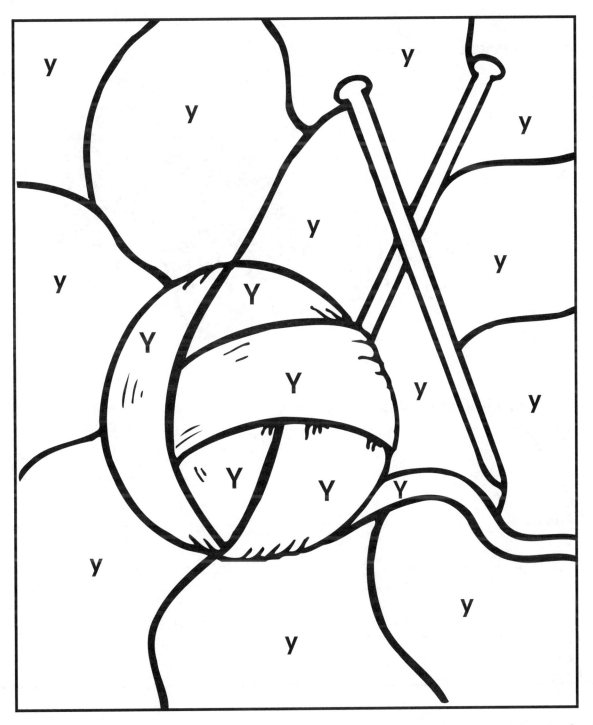

Letter Zz

Zz

Color the zinnias and the zebra.

Print the uppercase "Z."

Print the lowercase "z."

Letter Zz

Color the uppercase letters green.
Color the lowercase letters brown.

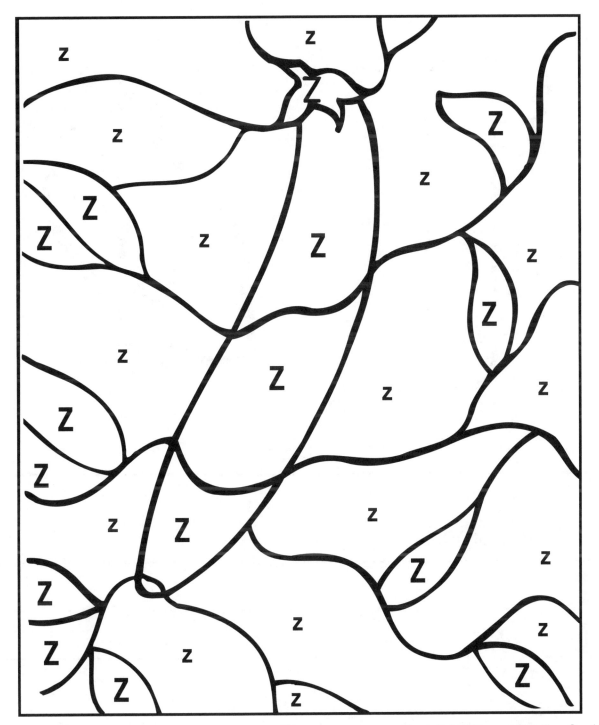

Essential Skills and Practice Grade PK

Name _____

1 One

Color "1" duck.

Print the numeral "1."

1
↓

Essential Skills and Practice Grade PK

Circle each "1."

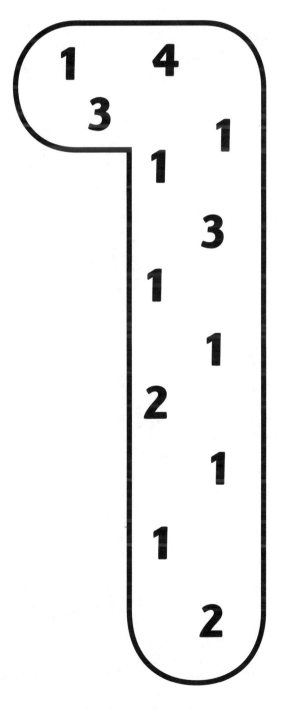

Essential Skills and Practice Grade PK

1 One

Color "1" balloon.

Essential Skills and Practice Grade PK

How Many?

How many in each box?

Essential Skills and Practice Grade PK

2 Two

Color "2" cats.

Print the numeral "2."

_____

Circle each "2."

Essential Skills and Practice Grade PK

2 Two

Color "2" kittens.

Essential Skills and Practice Grade PK

How Many?

How many in each box?

Essential Skills and Practice Grade PK

Number Review

Color the correct number.

1	🧸 🧸 🧸
2	🥁 🥁 🥁
3	🪆 🪆 🪆
1	⚪ ⚪ ⚪
2	🚐 🚐 🚐
3	▫G ▫G ▫G
1	✈ ✈ ✈

3 Three

Color "3" dogs.

Print the numeral "3."

Circle each "3."

Essential Skills and Practice Grade PK

Color "3" balls.

How Many?

How many in each box?

Number Review

Color the correct number.

1	
2	
3	
1	
2	
3	
1	

Essential Skills and Practice Grade PK

Color by Number

Color "1" red.
Color "2" yellow.
Color "3" blue.

Essential Skills and Practice Grade PK

4 Four

Color "4" animals.

Print the numeral "4."

Name _____

Circle each "4."

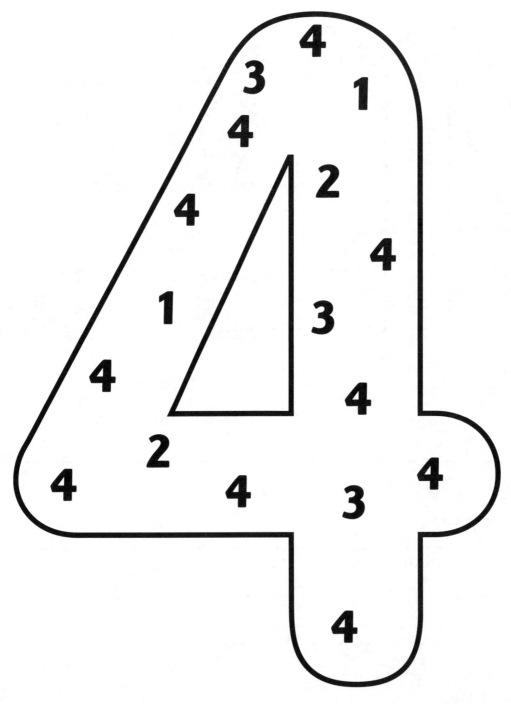

Essential Skills and Practice Grade PK

Color "4" rabbits.

Essential Skills and Practice Grade PK

How Many?

How many in each box?

Color by Number

Color "1" yellow.   Color "3" white.
Color "2" red.   Color "4" blue.

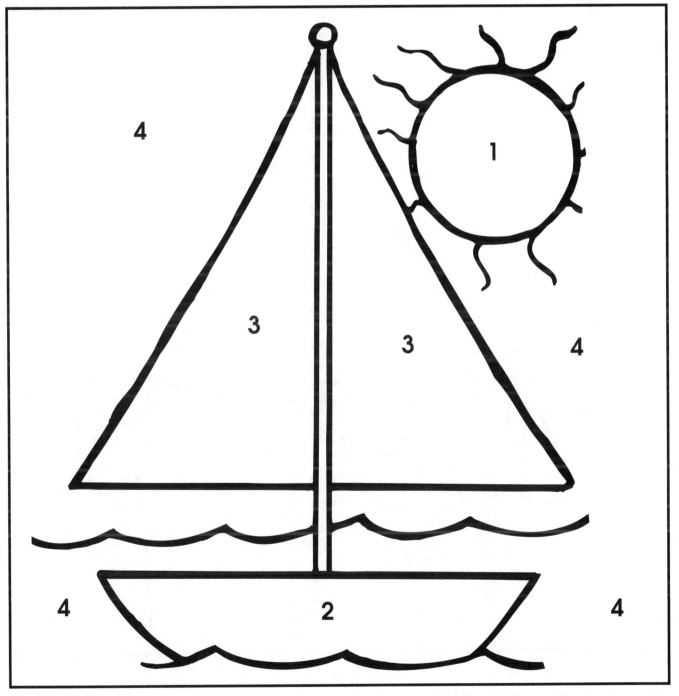

Dot-to-Dot

1 to 4

2 ●   ● 3

1   4

Essential Skills and Practice Grade PK

5 Five

Color "5" chicks.

Print the numeral "5."

Circle each "5."

Essential Skills and Practice Grade PK

5 Five

Color "5" kites.

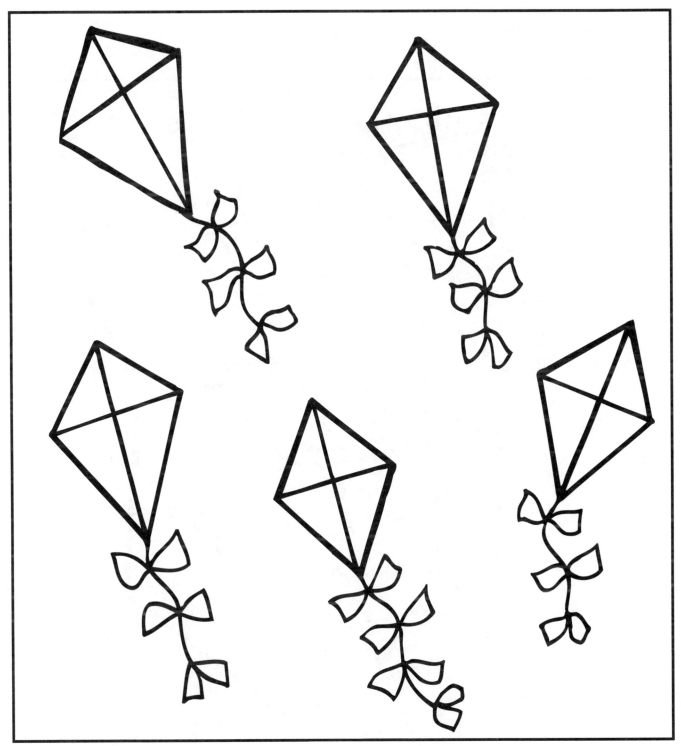

Essential Skills and Practice Grade PK

Color by Number

Color "1" yellow.   Color "4" red.
Color "2" purple.   Color "5" blue.
Color "3" green.

Essential Skills and Practice Grade PK

Dot-to-Dot

1 to 5

1 •• 5

• 4

2 •

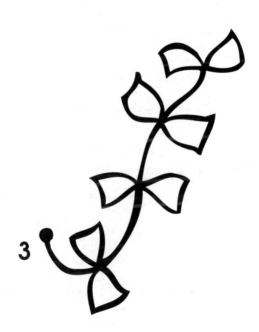

3 •

81 *Essential Skills and Practice Grade PK*

6 Six

Color "6" turtles.

Print the numeral "6."

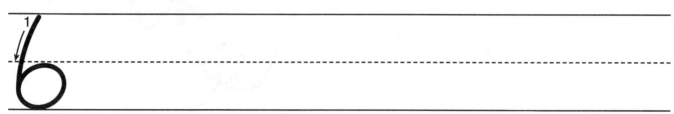

Circle each "6."

Essential Skills and Practice Grade PK

Color "6" frogs.

Essential Skills and Practice Grade PK

How Many?

How many in each box?

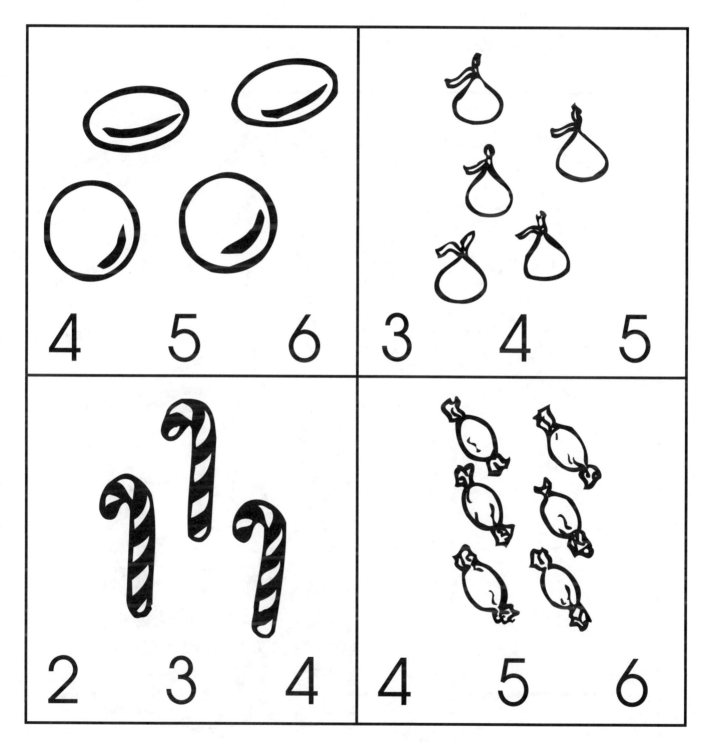

Essential Skills and Practice Grade PK

Color by Number

Color "1" brown.   Color "4" blue.
Color "2" yellow.   Color "5" red.
Color "3" orange.   Color "6" green.

Essential Skills and Practice Grade PK

Dot-to-Dot

1 to 6

2
●

4
●

5
●

3
●

1   **6**

Essential Skills and Practice Grade PK

7 Seven

Color "7" butterflies.

Print the numeral "7."

Circle each "7."

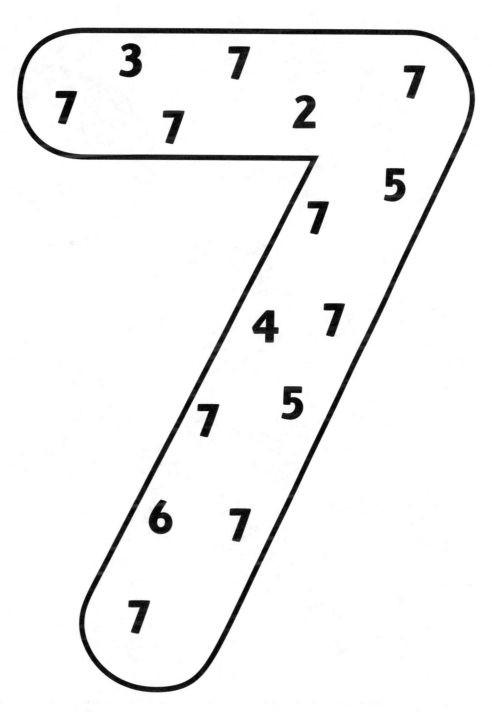

Essential Skills and Practice Grade PK

7 Seven

Color "7" fish.

Essential Skills and Practice Grade PK

Name _____

How Many?

How many in each box?

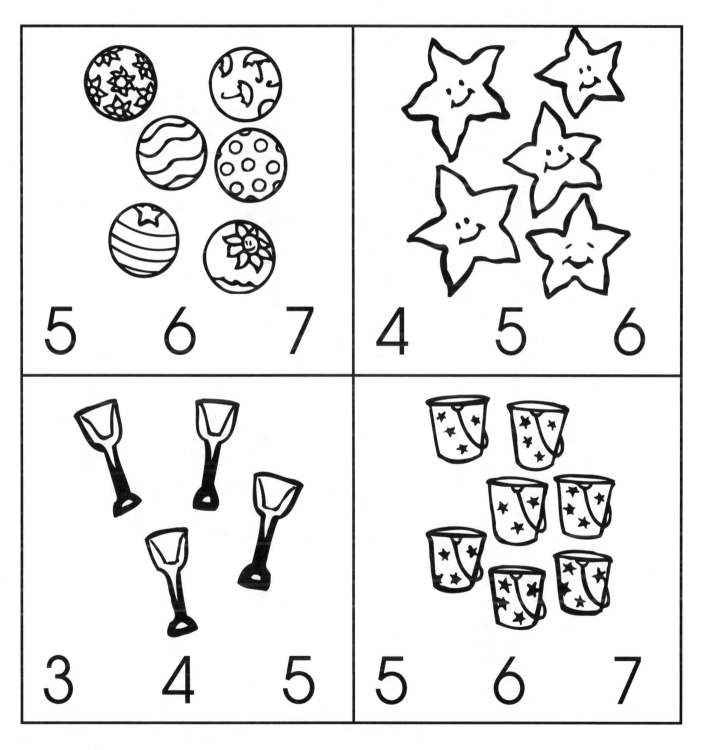

Essential Skills and Practice Grade PK

Color by Number

Color "1" yellow. Color "4" green. Color "7" orange.
Color "2" purple. Color "5" blue.
Color "3" brown. Color "6" red.

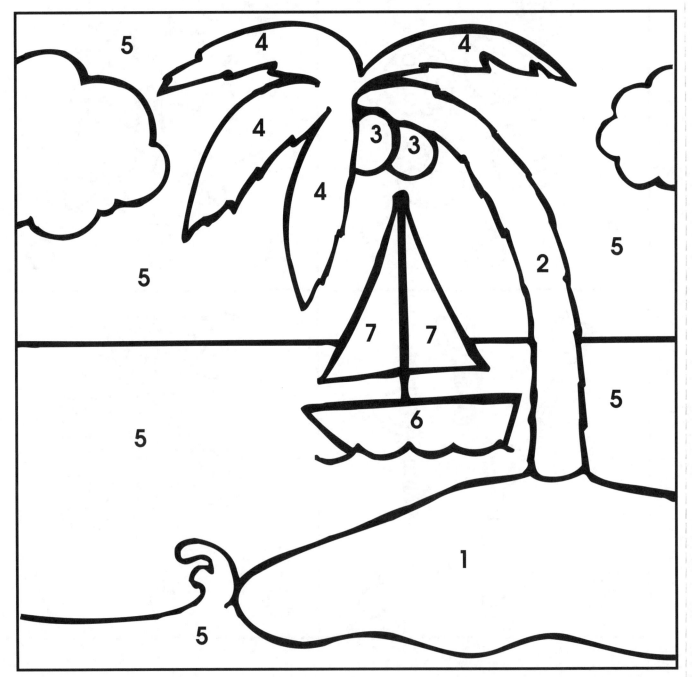

Essential Skills and Practice Grade PK

Dot-to-Dot

1 to 7

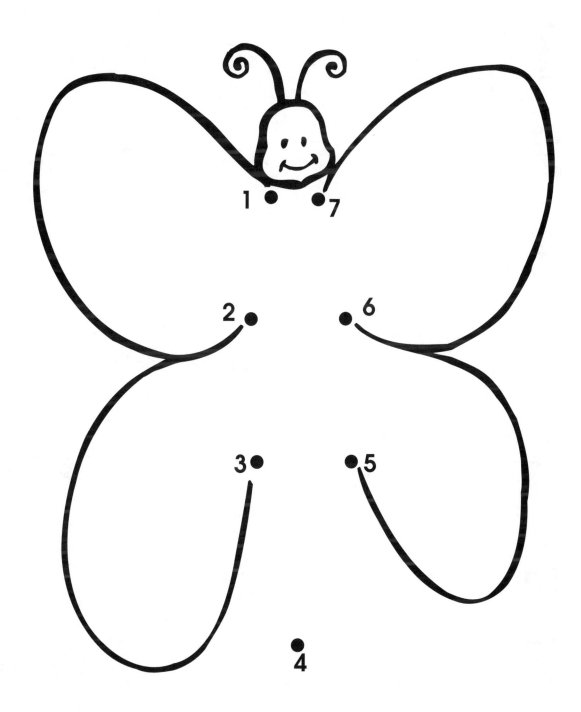

Essential Skills and Practice Grade PK

Number Review

Match the numeral to the set.
Draw a line.

1   ❤

2   ✿ ✿ ✿ ✿ ✿ ✿

3   ✲ ✲

4   ✳ ✳ ✳ ✳ ✳ ✳ ✳

5   ◆ ◆ ◆ ◆

6   ❖ ❖ ❖

7   ★ ★ ★ ★ ★

8 Eight

Color "8" bees.

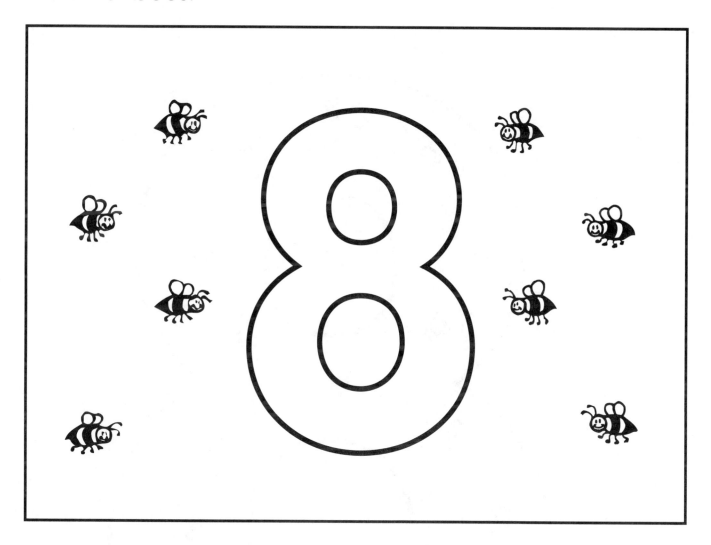

Print the numeral "8."

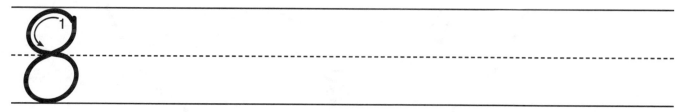

Name _____

Circle each "8."

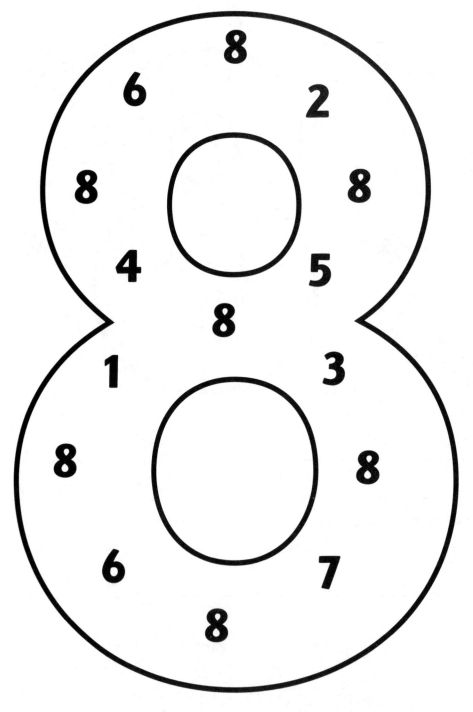

Essential Skills and Practice Grade PK

8 Eight

Color "8" bugs.

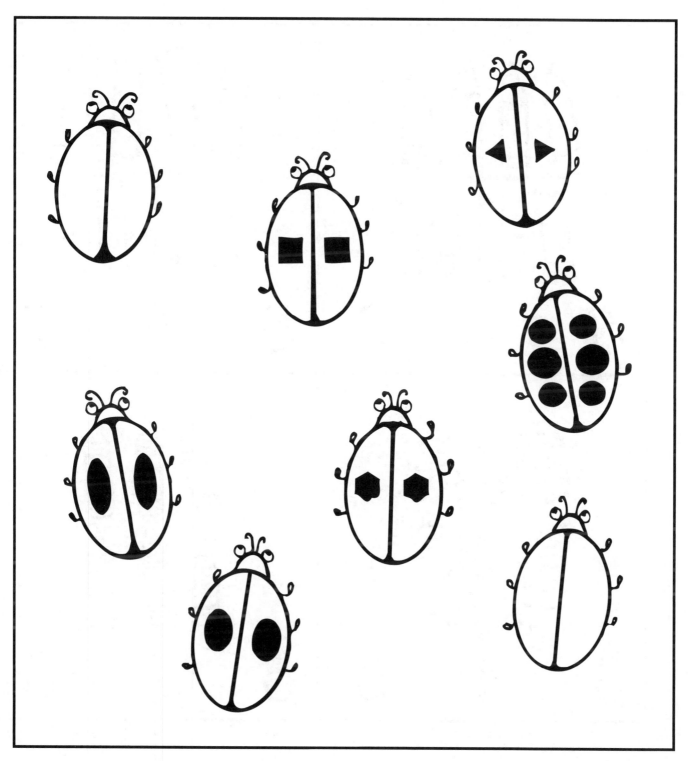

How Many?

How many in each box?

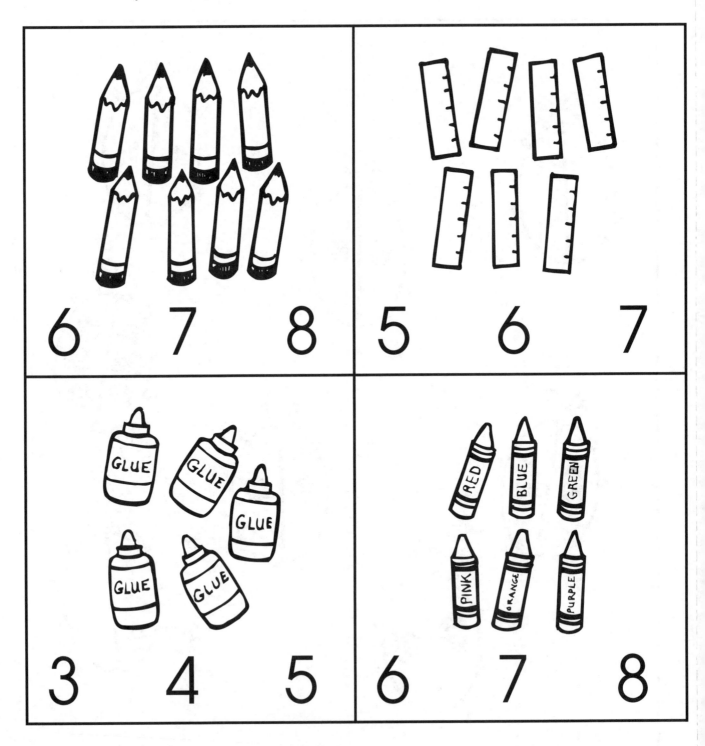

Essential Skills and Practice Grade PK

Color by Number

Color "1" gray.   Color "4" red.   Color "7" yellow.
Color "2" green.   Color "5" orange.   Color "8" blue.
Color "3" tan.   Color "6" brown.

Essential Skills and Practice Grade PK

Dot-to-Dot

1 to 8

1 8

7

2

3   6

4

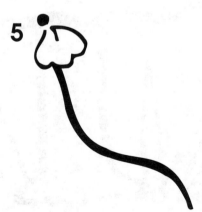

5

Number Review

Match the numeral to the set.
Draw a line.

1

2

3

4

5

6

7

8

◆◆◆◆◆

□□

●

▲▲▲▲▲▲▲▲

○○○

■■■■

□□□□□□□□

★★★★★★

Essential Skills and Practice Grade PK

9 Nine

Color "9" ladybugs.

Print the numeral "9."

Circle each "9."

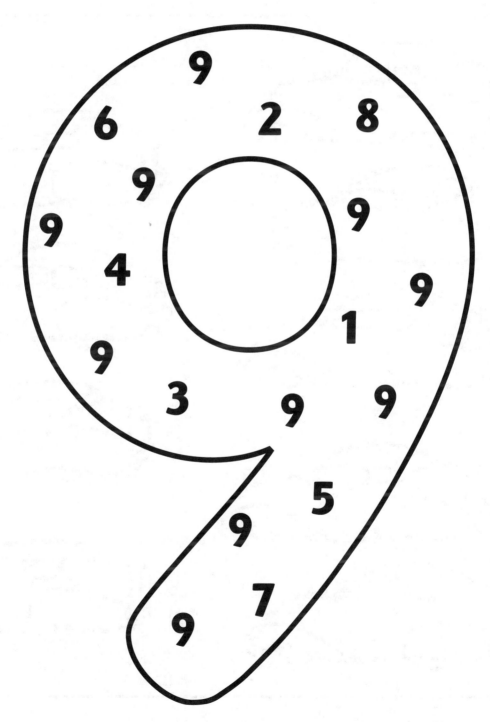

Essential Skills and Practice Grade PK

9 Nine

Color "9" cars.

How Many?

How many in each box?

7 8 9	6 7 8
5 6 7	7 8 9

Name _____

Color by Number

Color "1" white.   Color "4" green.   Color "7" pink.
Color "2" brown.   Color "5" red.   Color "8" blue.
Color "3" orange.   Color "6" purple.   Color "9" yellow.

    Essential Skills and Practice Grade PK

Dot-to-Dot

1 to 9

Essential Skills and Practice Grade PK

Number Review

Match the numeral to the set.
Draw a line.

1

2

3

4

5

6

7

8

9

Essential Skills and Practice Grade PK

10 Ten

Color "10" chipmunks.

Print the numeral "10."

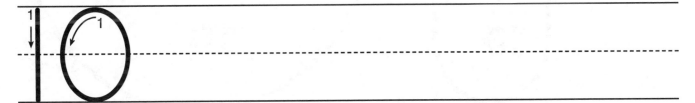

Essential Skills and Practice Grade PK

Circle each "10."

Essential Skills and Practice Grade PK

10 Ten

Color "10" puppies.

Essential Skills and Practice Grade PK

How Many?

How many in each box?

8 9 10	7 8 9
6 7 8	8 9 10

Essential Skills and Practice Grade PK

Number Review

Color the correct number.

10	🐰 ✏️ 👣 🐞 ⭐ 🌙 🎈 🍐 🍌 🍎
8	🐰 ✏️ 👣 🐞 ⭐ 🌙 🎈 🍐 🍌 🍎
6	🐰 ✏️ 👣 🐞 ⭐ 🌙 🎈 🍐 🍌 🍎
4	🐰 ✏️ 👣 🐞 ⭐ 🌙 🎈 🍐 🍌 🍎
2	🐰 ✏️ 👣 🐞 ⭐ 🌙 🎈 🍐 🍌 🍎
10	🐰 ✏️ 👣 🐞 ⭐ 🌙 🎈 🍐 🍌 🍎
7	🐰 ✏️ 👣 🐞 ⭐ 🌙 🎈 🍐 🍌 🍎

Essential Skills and Practice Grade PK

Color by Number

Color "1 "red.
Color "2" yellow.
Color "3" blue.
Color "4" green.

Color "5" orange.
Color "6" purple.
Color "7" black.

Color "8" brown.
Color "9" pink.
Color "10" gray.

Essential Skills and Practice Grade PK

Dot-to-Dot

1 to 10

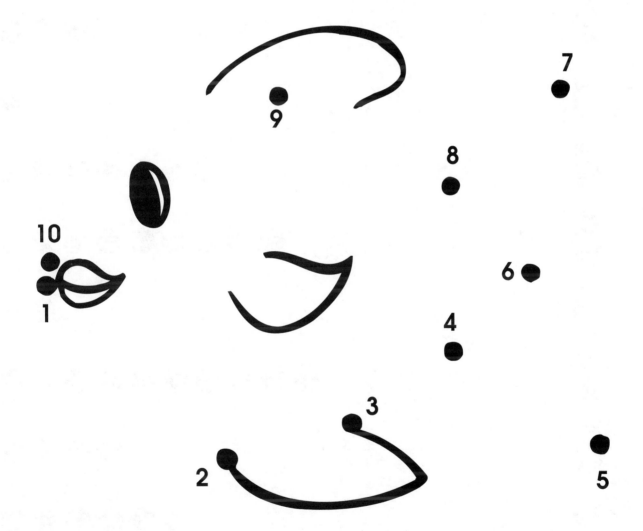

Essential Skills and Practice Grade PK

Number Review

Match the numeral to the set.
Draw a line.

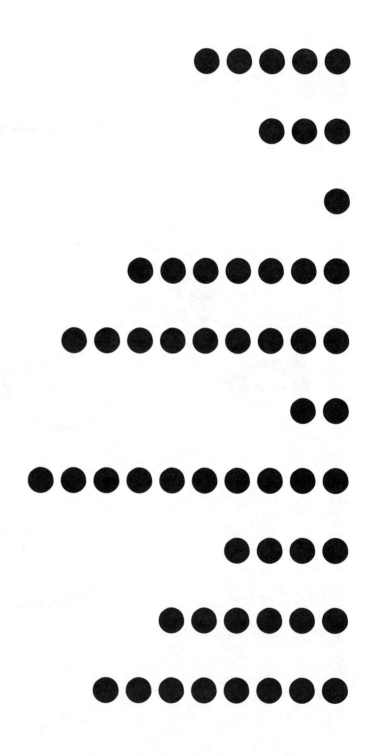

1
2
3
4
5
6
7
8
9
10

Essential Skills and Practice Grade PK

Red

Color the apple red.

Essential Skills and Practice Grade PK

Which objects do you think should be red?

Essential Skills and Practice Grade PK

Color the apple red.

Trace the word. Print the word.

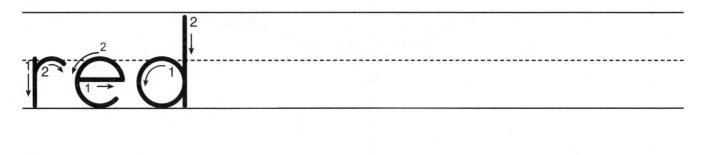

Essential Skills and Practice Grade PK

Read the words. Color the picture.

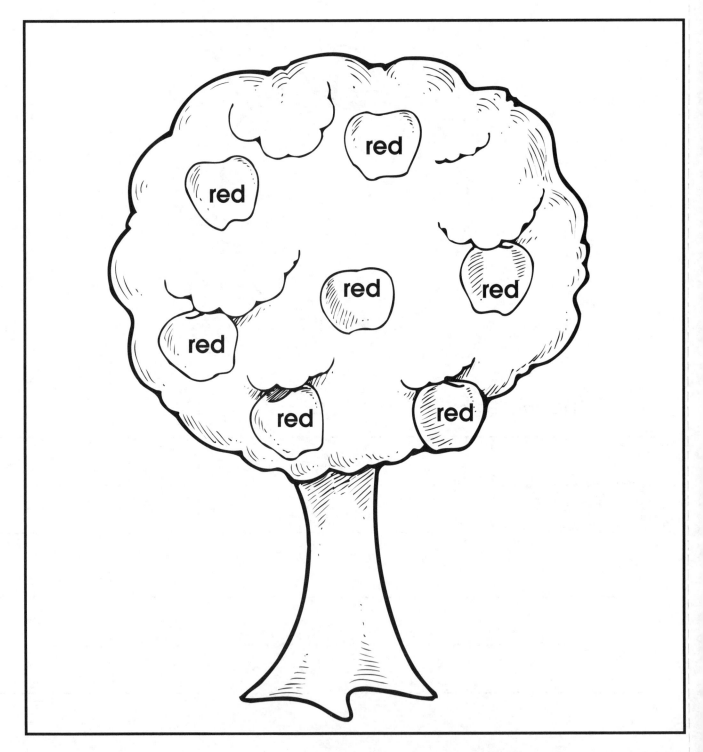

Essential Skills and Practice Grade PK

Blue

Color the ball blue.

Essential Skills and Practice Grade PK

Which objects do you think should be blue?

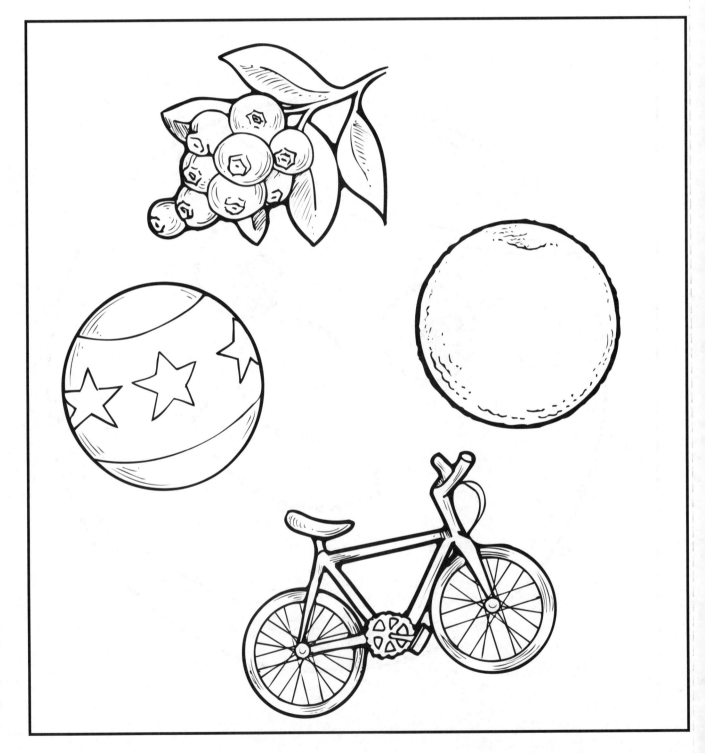

Color the ball blue.

Trace the word. Print the word.

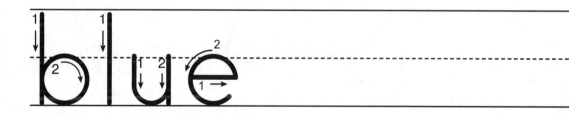

Color Review

Read the words. Color the picture.

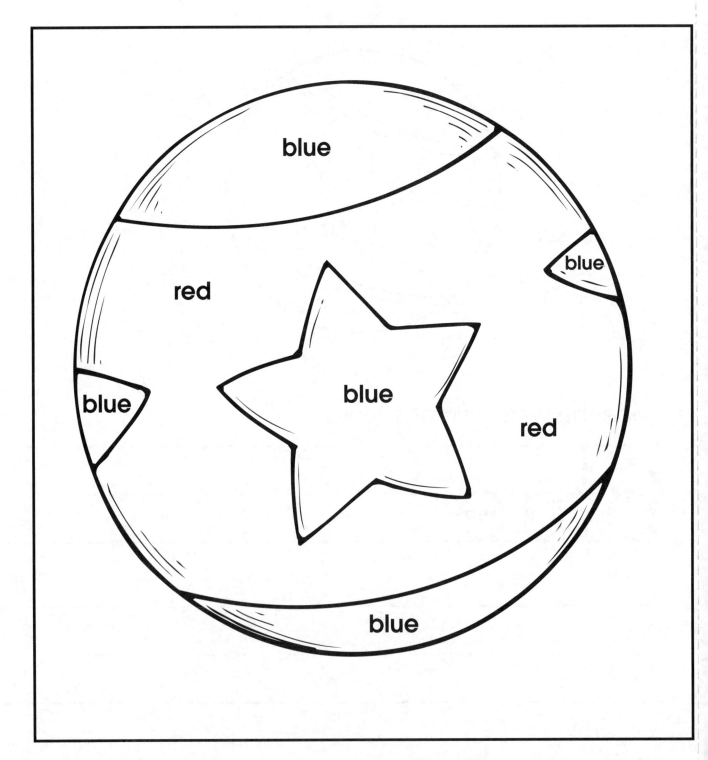

Essential Skills and Practice Grade PK

Yellow

Color the sun yellow.

Essential Skills and Practice Grade PK

Which objects do you think should be yellow?

Essential Skills and Practice Grade PK

Color the sun yellow.

Trace the word. Print the word.

Read the words. Color the picture.

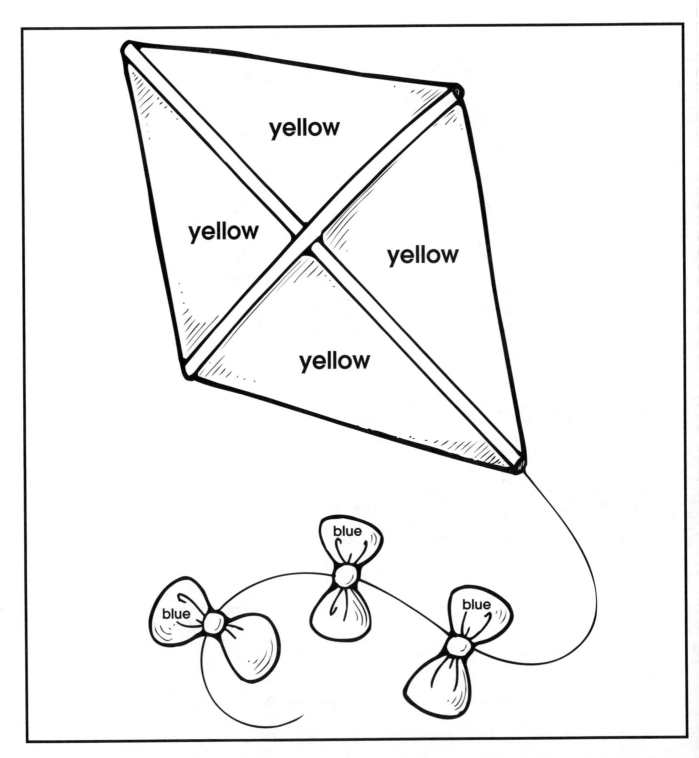

Essential Skills and Practice Grade PK

Color Review

Draw a line to match the picture to the color word.

red

blue

yellow

Green

Color the frog green.

Essential Skills and Practice Grade PK

Which objects do you think should be green?

Essential Skills and Practice Grade PK

Color the frog green.

Trace the word. Print the word.

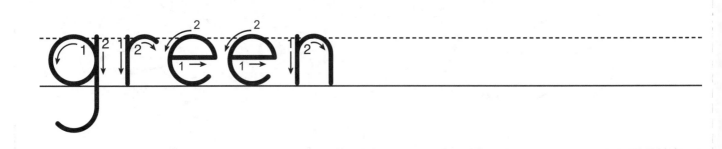

Essential Skills and Practice Grade PK

Color Review

Read the words. Color the picture.

Essential Skills and Practice Grade PK

Orange

Color the pumpkin orange.

Essential Skills and Practice Grade PK

Which objects do you think should be orange?

Essential Skills and Practice Grade PK

Color the pumpkin orange.

Trace the word. Print the word.

Essential Skills and Practice Grade PK

Name _____

Color Review

Read the words. Color the picture.

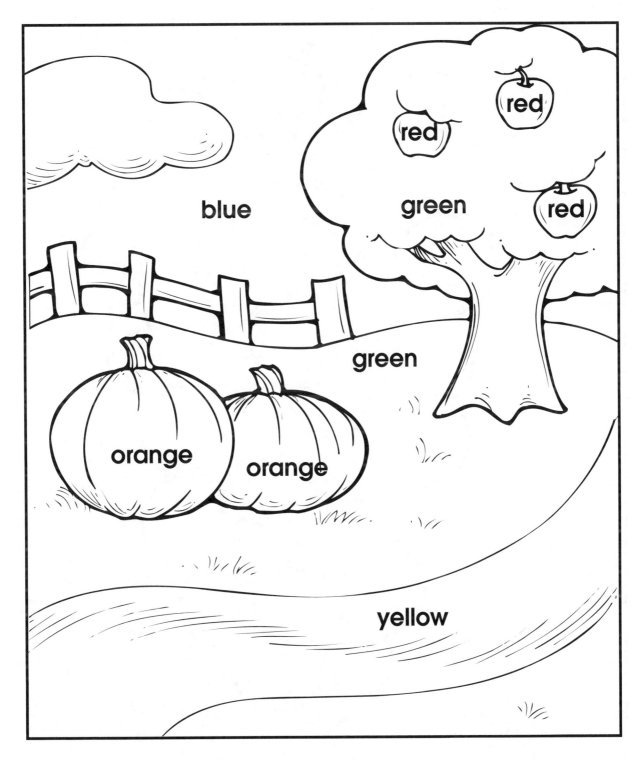

Essential Skills and Practice Grade PK

Purple

Color the grapes purple.

Essential Skills and Practice Grade PK

Which objects do you think should be purple?

Color the grapes purple.

Trace the word. Print the word.

purple

Essential Skills and Practice Grade PK

Color Review

Read the words. Color the picture.

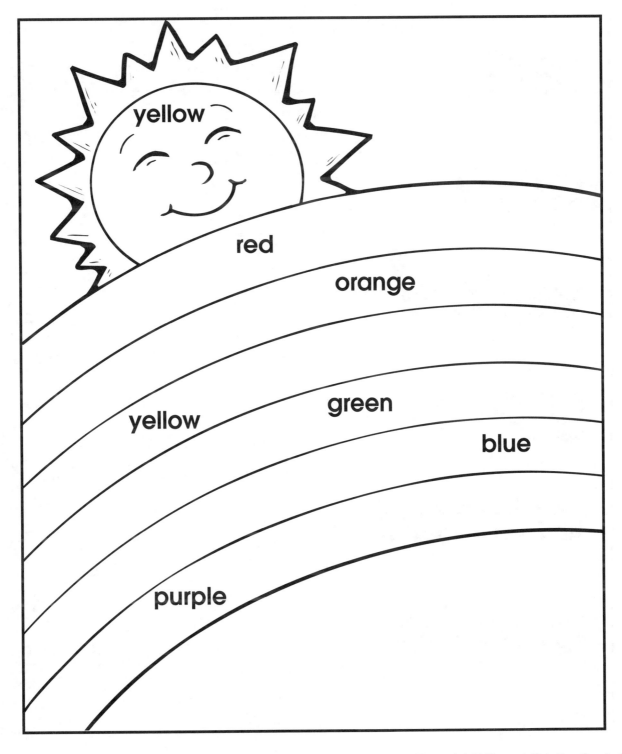

Essential Skills and Practice Grade PK

Draw a line to match the picture to the color word.

red

blue

yellow

green

orange

purple

Essential Skills and Practice Grade PK

Black

Color the ant black.

Essential Skills and Practice Grade PK

Which objects do you think should be black?

Essential Skills and Practice Grade PK

Color the ant black.

Trace the word. Print the word.

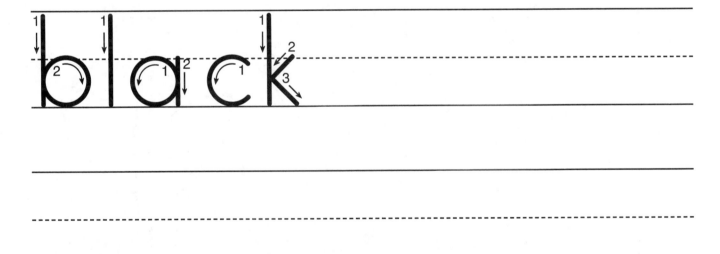

Essential Skills and Practice Grade PK

Color Review

Read the words. Color the picture.

Essential Skills and Practice Grade PK

Brown

Color the bear brown.

Essential Skills and Practice Grade PK

Which objects do you think should be brown?

Essential Skills and Practice Grade PK

Color the bear brown.

Trace the word. Print the word.

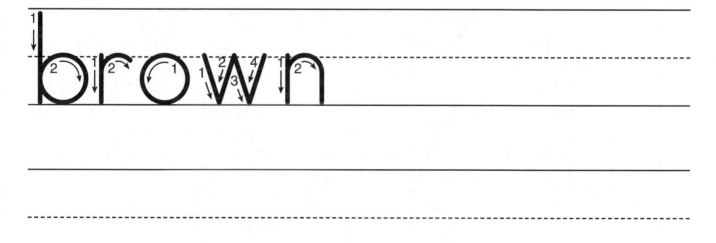

Essential Skills and Practice Grade PK

Color Review

Read the words. Color the picture.

Essential Skills and Practice Grade PK

White

Color the cloud white.

Essential Skills and Practice Grade PK

Which objects do you think should be white?

Essential Skills and Practice Grade PK

Color the cloud white.

Trace the word. Print the word.

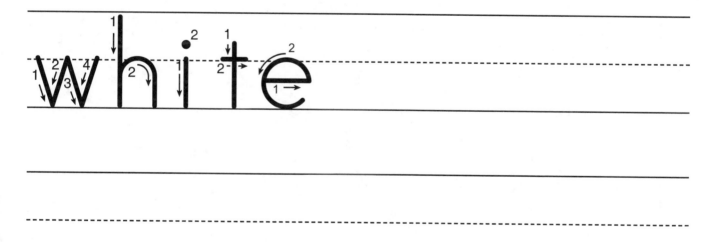

Color Review

Read the words. Color the picture

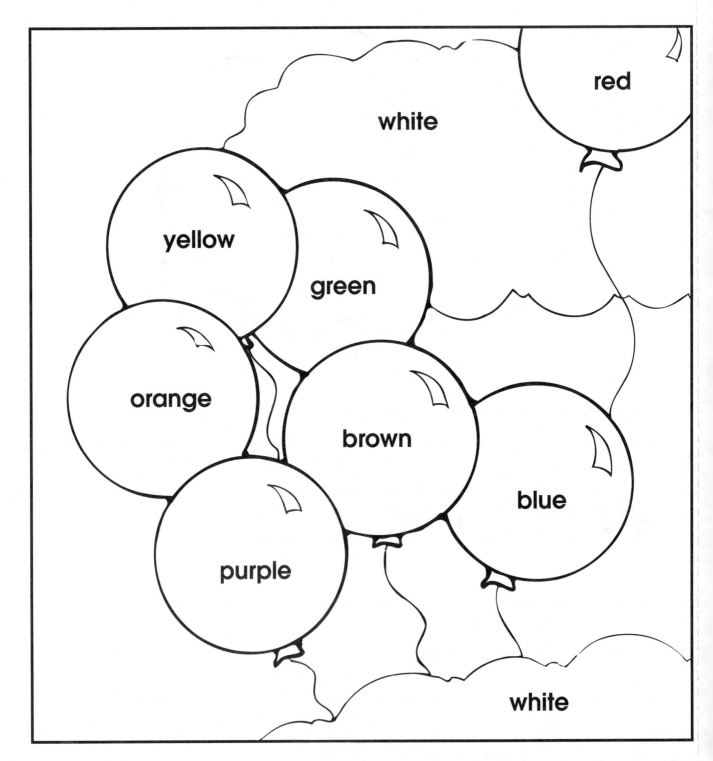

Essential Skills and Practice Grade PK

Pink

Color the pig pink.

Which objects do you think should be pink?

Essential Skills and Practice Grade PK

Color the pig pink.

Trace the word. Print the word.

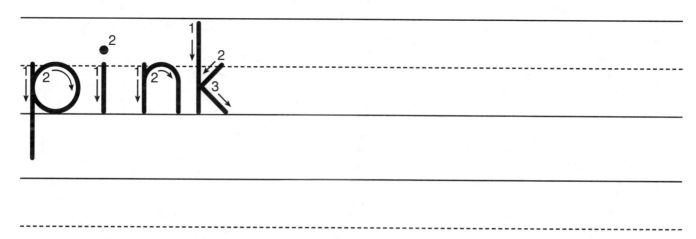

Essential Skills and Practice Grade PK

Color Review

Read the words. Color the picture.

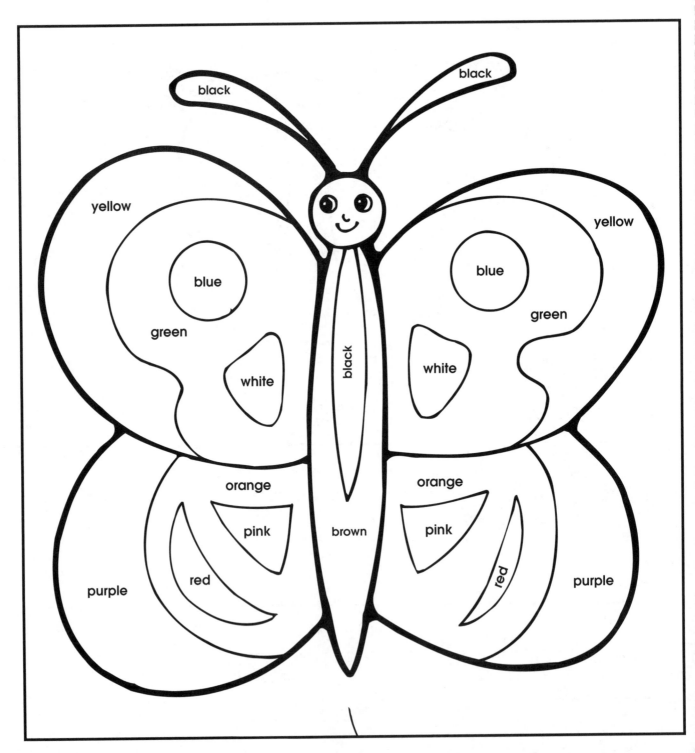

Draw a line to match the picture to the color word.

red

blue

yellow

green

orange

purple

black

brown

white

pink

Essential Skills and Practice Grade PK

Circle

Color the circle.

 Essential Skills and Practice Grade PK

Trace all the circles.

Essential Skills and Practice Grade PK

Color the circle.

Trace the word. Print the word.

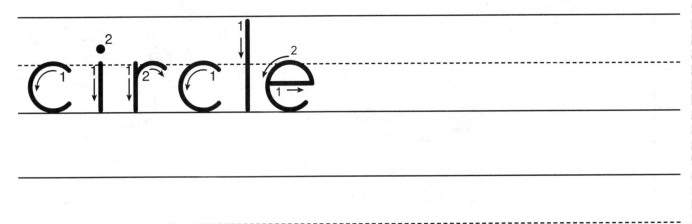

Can you find all the circles?

Essential Skills and Practice Grade PK

Square

Color the square.

Name _____

Trace all the squares.

Essential Skills and Practice Grade PK

Color the square.

Trace the word. Print the word.

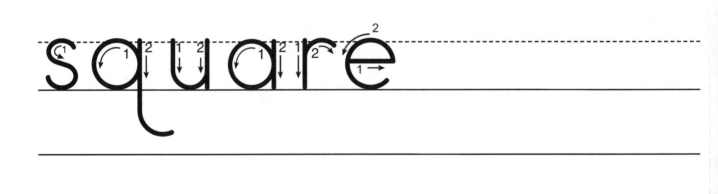

Can you find all the squares?

Essential Skills and Practice Grade PK

Triangle

Color the triangle.

 Essential Skills and Practice Grade PK

Name _____

Trace all the triangles.

Essential Skills and Practice Grade PK

Color the triangle.

Trace the word. Print the word.

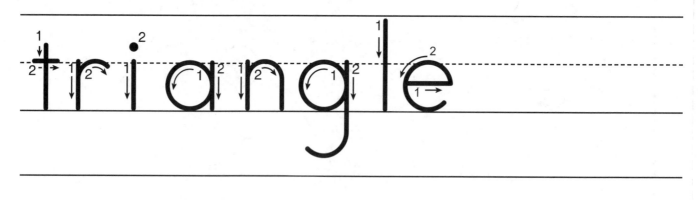

Can you find all the triangles?

171

Rectangle

Color the rectangle.

Essential Skills and Practice Grade PK

Trace all the rectangles.

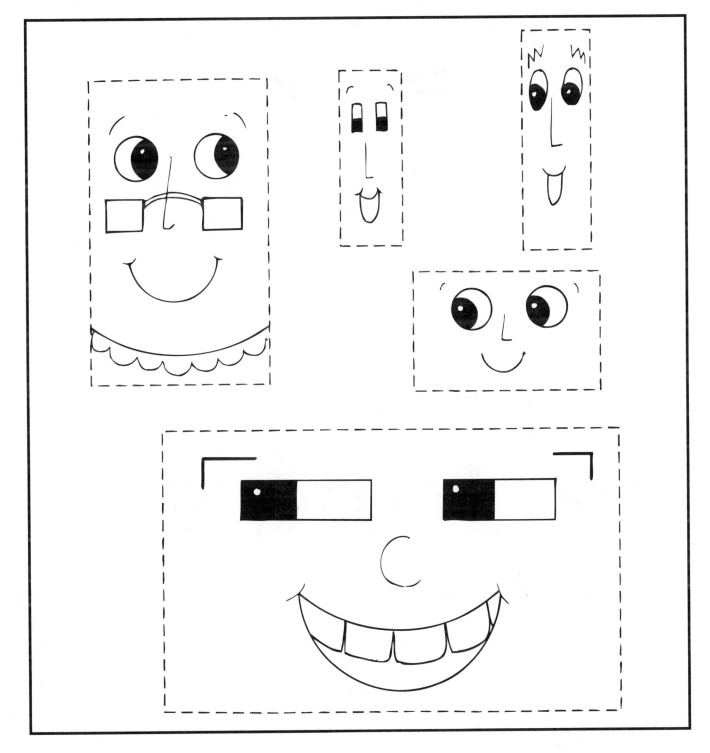

Essential Skills and Practice Grade PK

Color the rectangle.

Trace the word. Print the word.

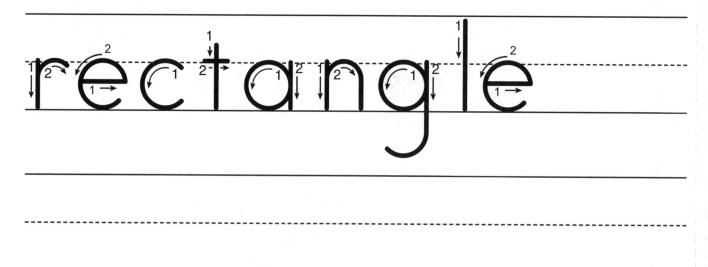

Can you find all the rectangles?

Essential Skills and Practice Grade PK

Name ______________________________

Shape Review

Draw a line from the word to the shape.

circle

square

triangle

rectangle

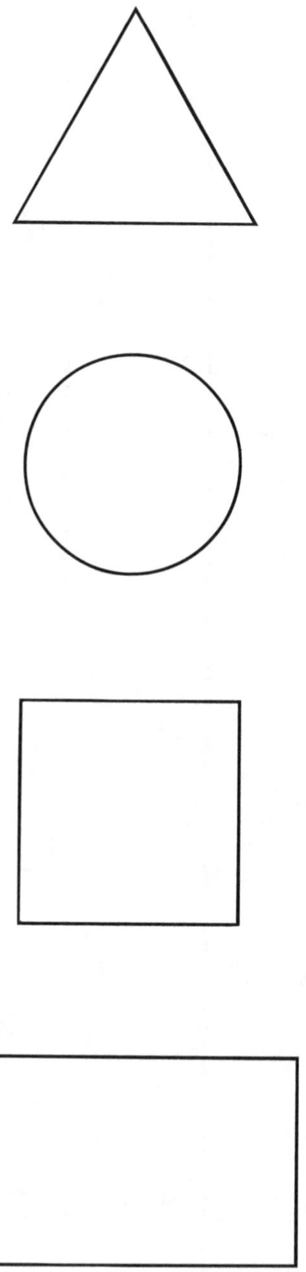

Diamond

Color the diamond.

Essential Skills and Practice Grade PK

Trace all the diamonds.

green

Essential Skills and Practice Grade PK

Color the diamond.

Trace the word. Print the word.

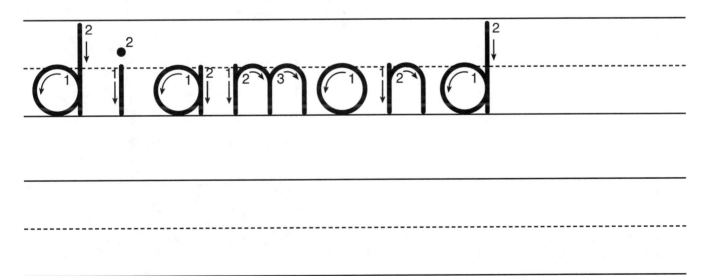

Essential Skills and Practice Grade PK

Can you find all the diamonds?

Essential Skills and Practice Grade PK

Star

Color the star.

Essential Skills and Practice Grade PK

Trace all the stars.

Essential Skills and Practice Grade PK

Color the star.

Trace the word. Print the word.

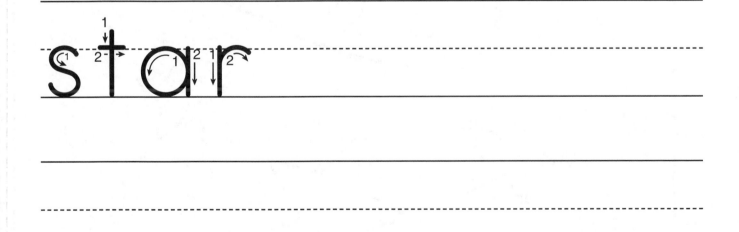

Can you find all the stars?

Octagon

Color the octagon.

Name _____

Trace all the octagons.

Essential Skills and Practice Grade PK

Color the octagon.

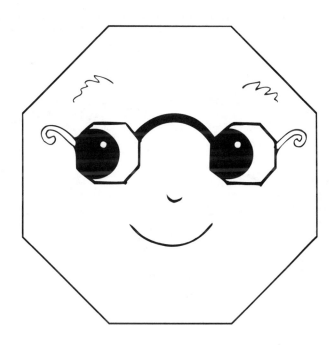

Trace the word. Print the word.

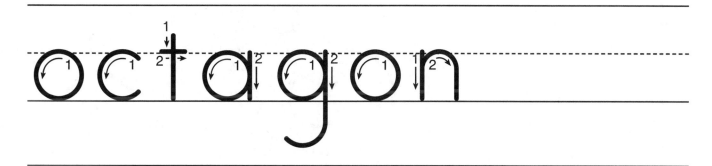

Can you find all the octagons?

Essential Skills and Practice Grade PK

Oval

Color the oval.

Essential Skills and Practice Grade PK

Trace all the ovals.

Essential Skills and Practice Grade PK

Color the oval.

Trace the word. Print the word.

oval

Can you find all the ovals?

Essential Skills and Practice Grade PK

Draw a line from the word to the shape.

circle

square

triangle

rectangle

diamond

octagon

star

oval

Essential Skills and Practice Grade PK

Alike or Different

Color the three that are alike in each row.

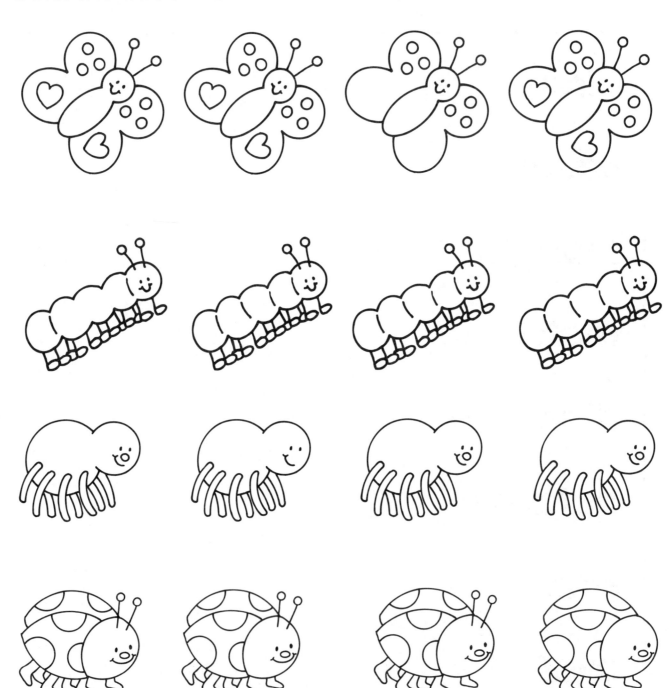

Alike or Different

Color the three that are alike in each row.

Essential Skills and Practice Grade PK

Animal Opposites

Draw a line from each animal to its opposite.

day   sad   wet   front

dry   back   happy   night

Essential Skills and Practice Grade PK

Seasons Opposites

Draw a line from each picture to its opposite.

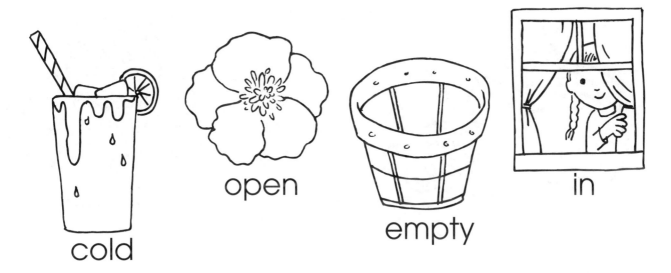

cold   open   empty   in

full   hot   out   close

Real and Not Real

Circle the animals that are real. Color.

Essential Skills and Practice Grade PK

Big and Small

Draw a line to the matching thing that is the same size.

Big and Little

Trace the words. Color the big things red. Color the little things blue.

little

big

Pet Shop Friends

Color the biggest.

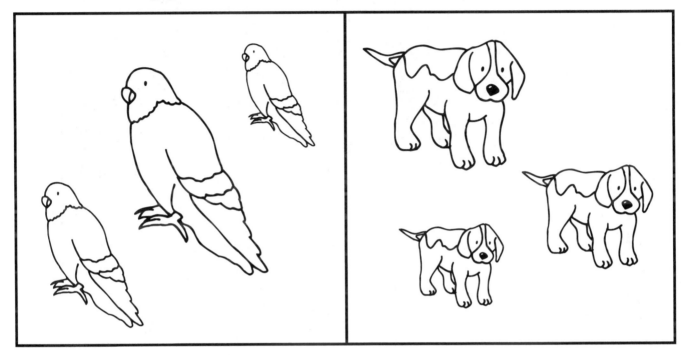

Color the smallest.

Name _____

Toys That Go

Color the biggest toy on each shelf red.
Color the smallest toy on each shelf blue.

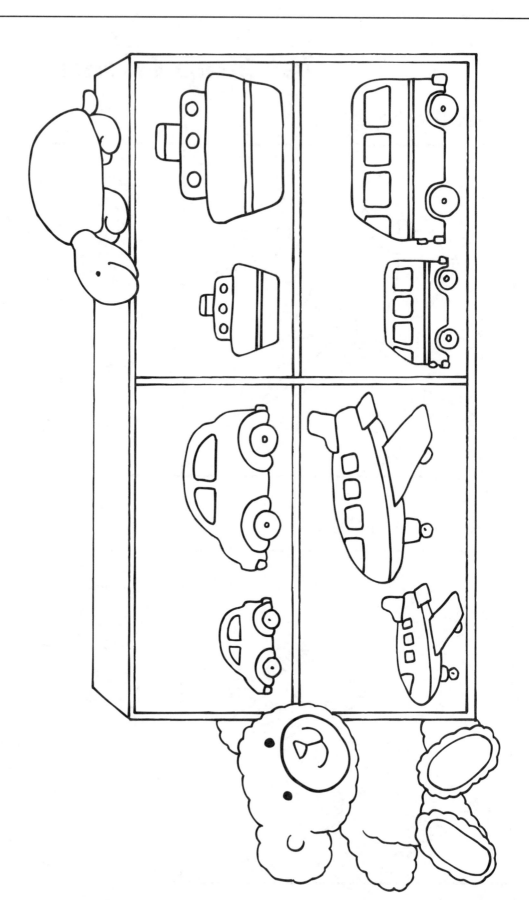

Essential Skills and Practice Grade PK

Long and Short

Trace the words. Color the short things green. Color the long things orange.

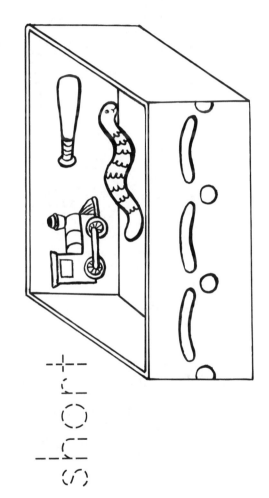

short

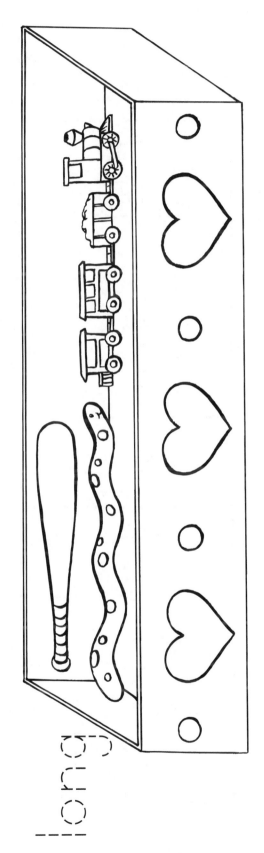

long

203

More or Less?

Circle the group in each box that has more.

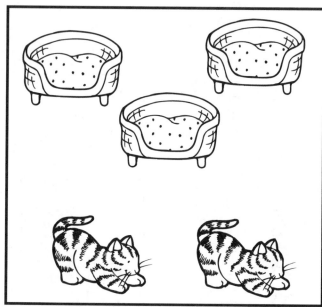

Circle the group in each box that has less.

Essential Skills and Practice Grade PK

More or Less?

Circle the group in each box that has more.

Circle the group in each box that has less.

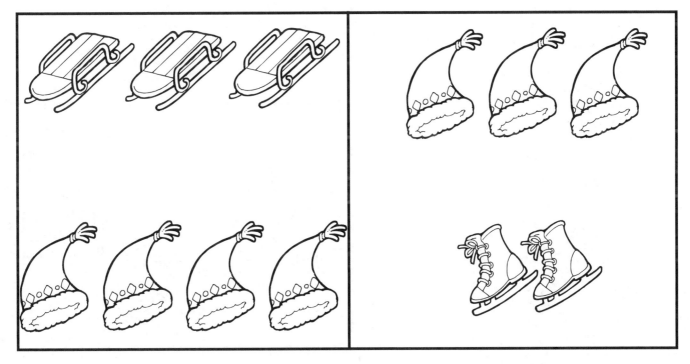

Essential Skills and Practice Grade PK

Where Do They Belong?

Draw a line from each object to its matching group.

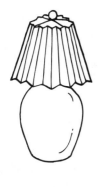

Name _____

Busy Days and Nights

Draw a line to what happens next. Color.

Essential Skills and Practice Grade PK

What Happens Next?

Draw a line to what happens next. Color.

Essential Skills and Practice Grade PK

Getting Along

Circle the pictures that show the better way to behave.

Essential Skills and Practice Grade PK

Hot or Cold?

Draw a line from each child to the correct picture.

Essential Skills and Practice Grade PK

Matching Clothes

Draw a line from each object to its matching group.

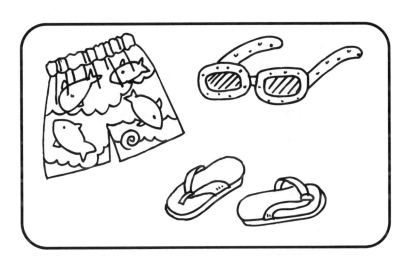

What Are They Wearing?

Draw a line to match each child's front and back.

 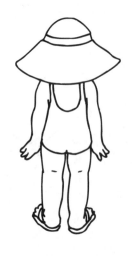  

Essential Skills and Practice Grade PK

What Do You Wear?

Draw a line from each piece of clothing to the child who is wearing it.

Essential Skills and Practice Grade PK

Going for a Ride

Connect the dots from **a** to **e**. Color the picture.

Essential Skills and Practice Grade PK

Wonderful Wind

Connect the dots from **a** to **e**. Color the picture.

Name _____

Up, Up, and Away

Connect the dots from **a** to **h**. Color the picture.

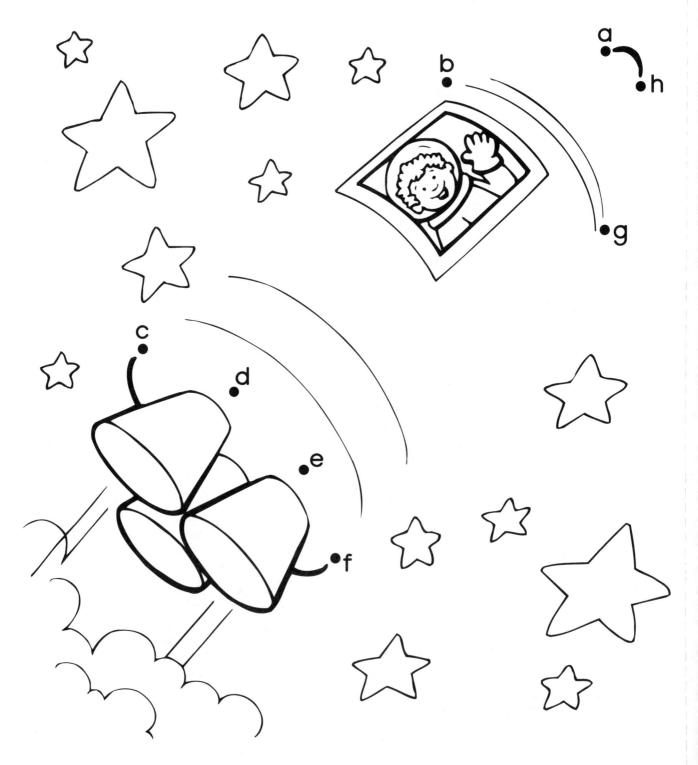

Essential Skills and Practice Grade PK

A Birthday Treat

Connect the dots from **a** to **i**. Color the picture.

Essential Skills and Practice Grade PK

Very, Very Tall

Connect the dots from **a** to **m**. Color the picture.

Shoot!

Connect the dots from **a** to **m**. Color the picture.

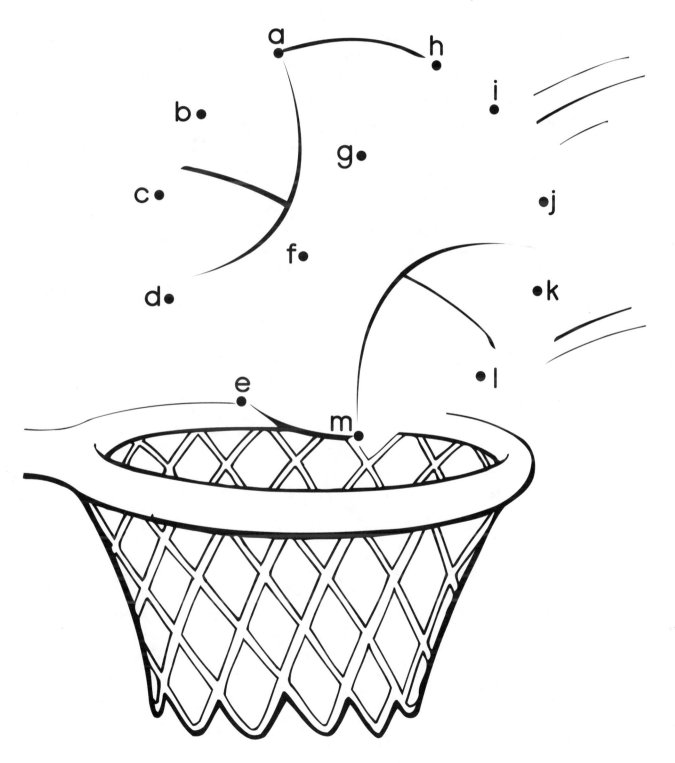

Essential Skills and Practice Grade PK

Surf's Up!

Connect the dots from **a** to **p**. Color the picture.

Home Sweet Home

Connect the dots from **a** to **p**. Color the picture.

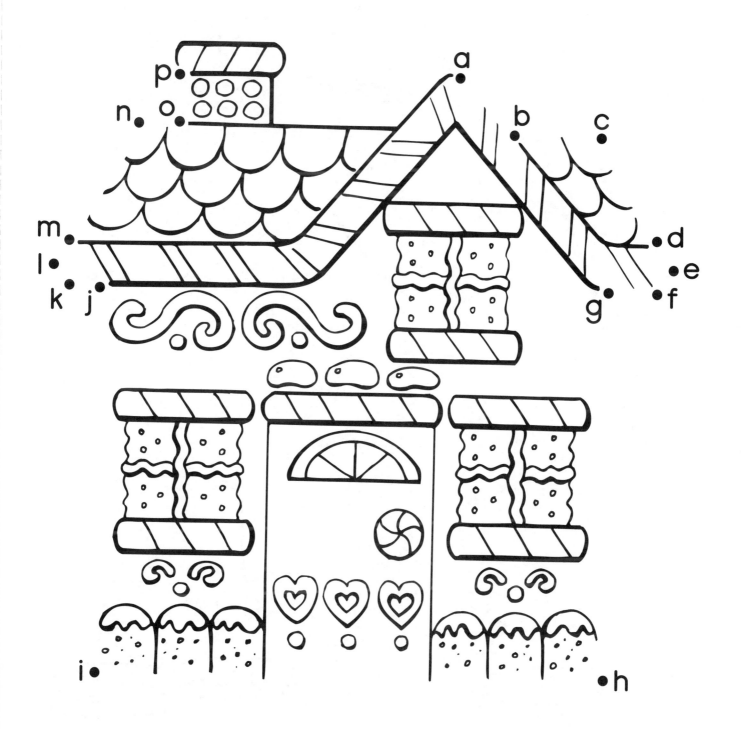

Essential Skills and Practice Grade PK

Name _____

Saving Up

Connect the dots from **a** to **t**. Color the picture.

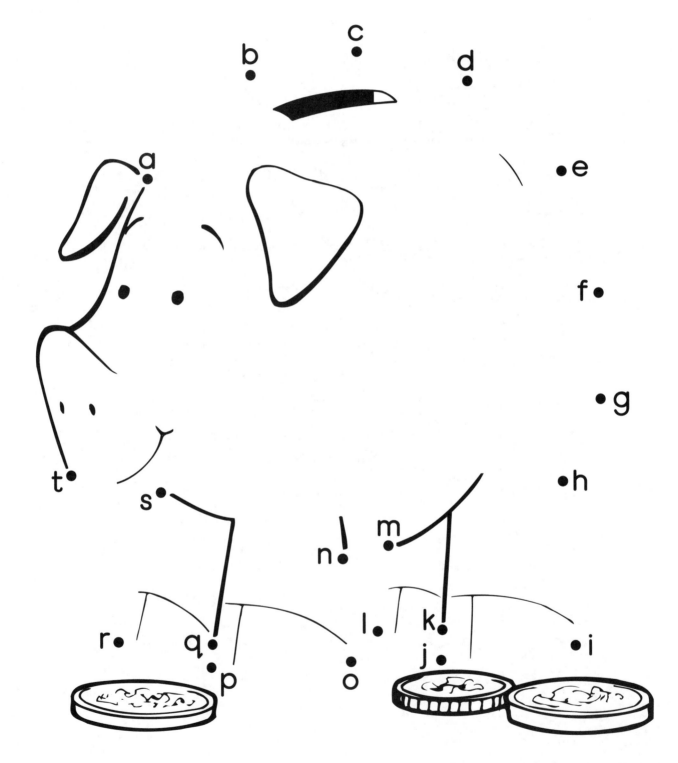

Name _____

Racing Around

Connect the dots from **a** to **t**. Color the picture.

Essential Skills and Practice Grade PK

Water Hunter

Connect the dots from **a** to **z**. Color the picture.

A Cool Treat

Connect the dots from **a** to **z**. Color the picture.

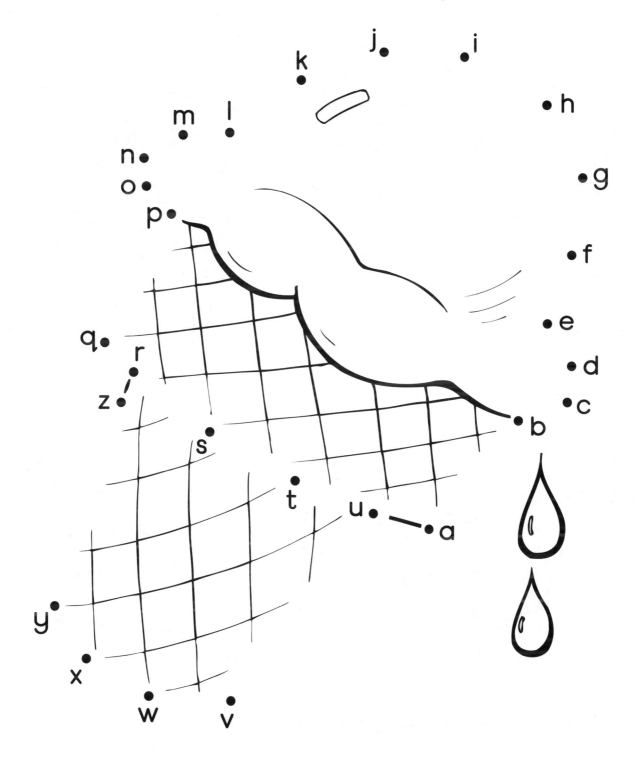

Essential Skills and Practice Grade PK

Walrus

Connect the dots from **a** to **z**. Color the picture.

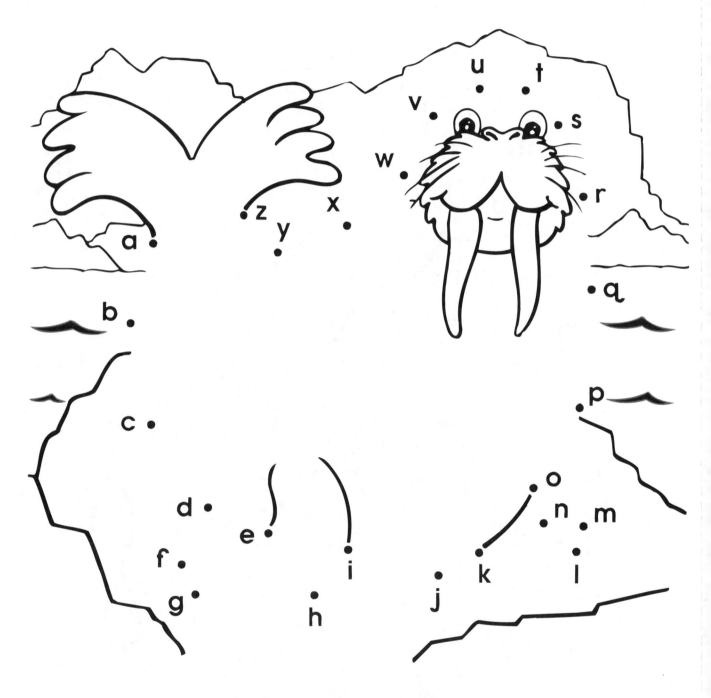

I use my tusks as hooks to climb on ice.

Sea Horse

Connect the dots from **a** to **z**. Color the picture.

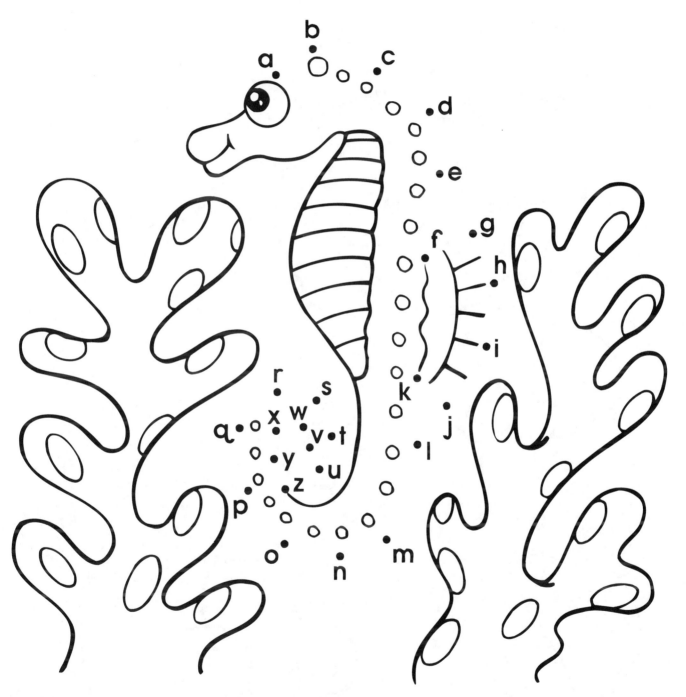

I use my tail to cling to sea plants.

Essential Skills and Practice Grade PK

Let's Play

Connect the dots from **A** to **E**. Color the picture.

Essential Skills and Practice Grade PK

A Hungry Kitten

Connect the dots from **A** to **E**. Color the picture.

Growing Time

Connect the dots from **A** to **H**. Color the picture.

Essential Skills and Practice Grade PK

Lost in the Grass

Connect the dots from **A** to **H**. Color the picture.

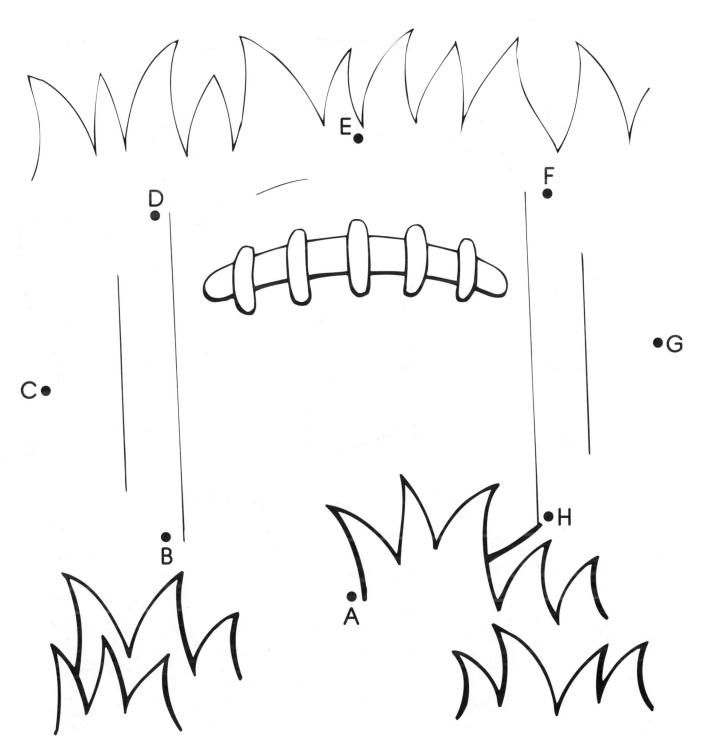

Essential Skills and Practice Grade PK

A Good Little Swimmer

Connect the dots from **A** to **M**. Color the picture.

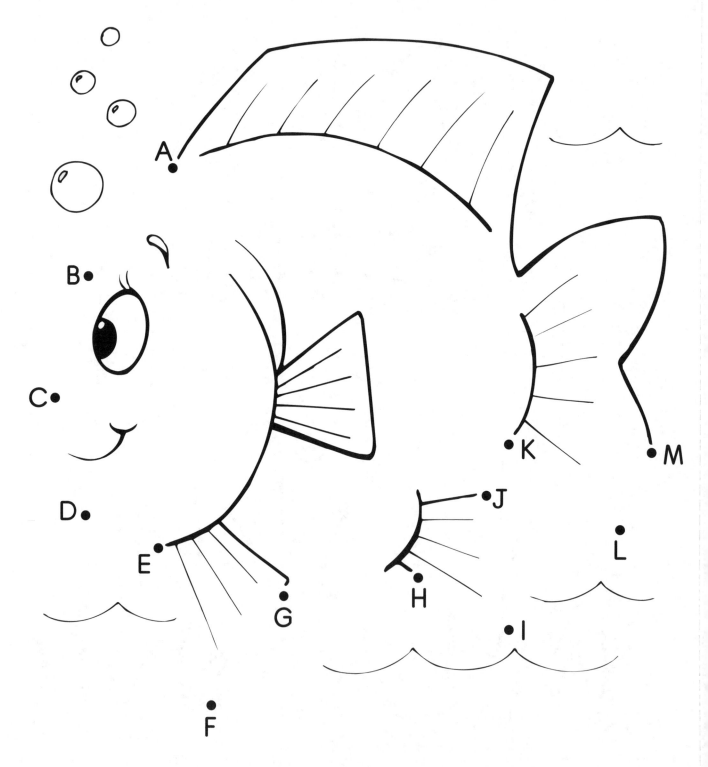

Essential Skills and Practice Grade PK

A Favorite Toy

Connect the dots from **A** to **M**. Color the picture.

Load It Up

Connect the dots from **A** to **N**. Color the picture.

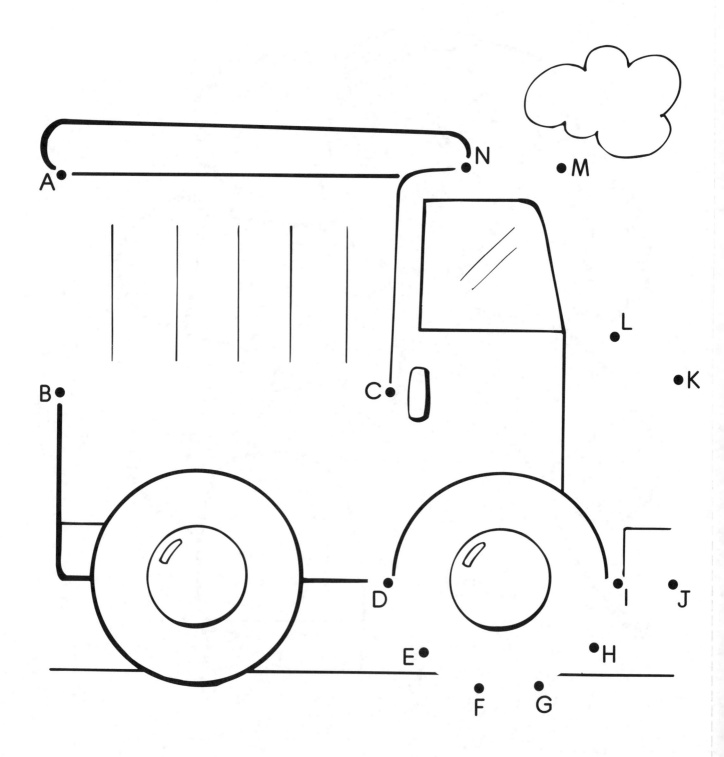

Essential Skills and Practice Grade PK

Silly Spider

Connect the dots from **A** to **P**. Color the picture.

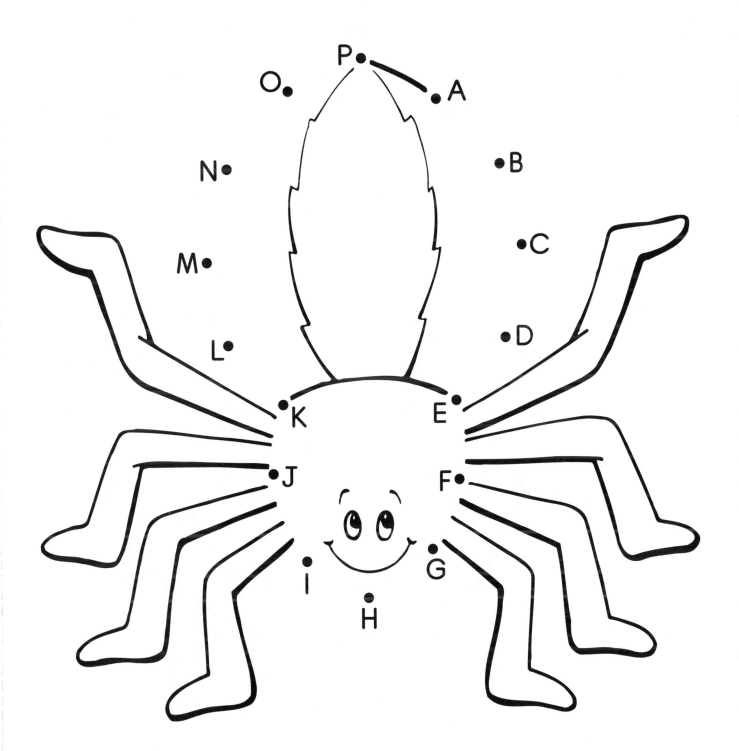

Essential Skills and Practice Grade PK

Game Time

Connect the dots from **A** to **P**. Color the picture.

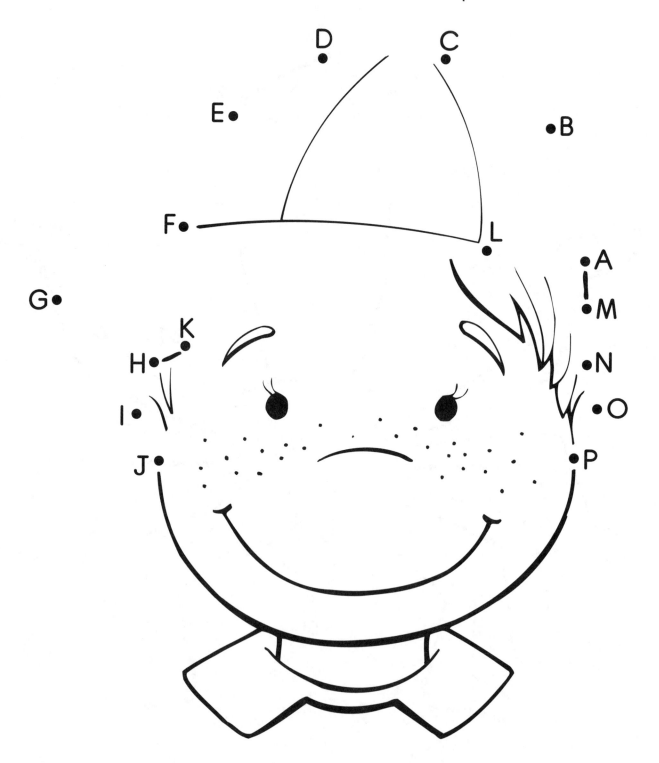

Essential Skills and Practice Grade PK

Sailing Around

Connect the dots from **A** to **T**. Color the picture.

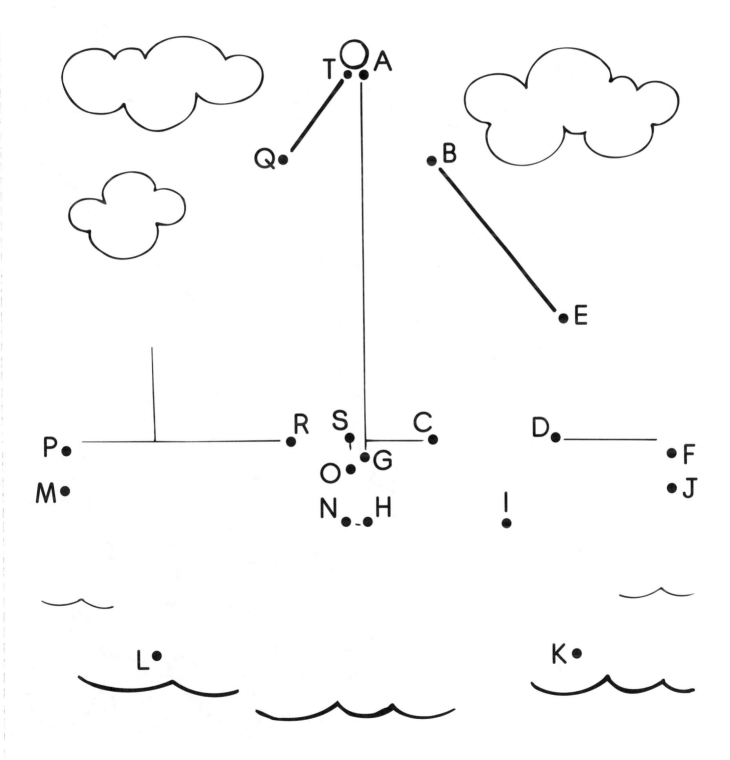

Essential Skills and Practice Grade PK

Busy Bees

Connect the dots from **A** to **T**. Color the picture.

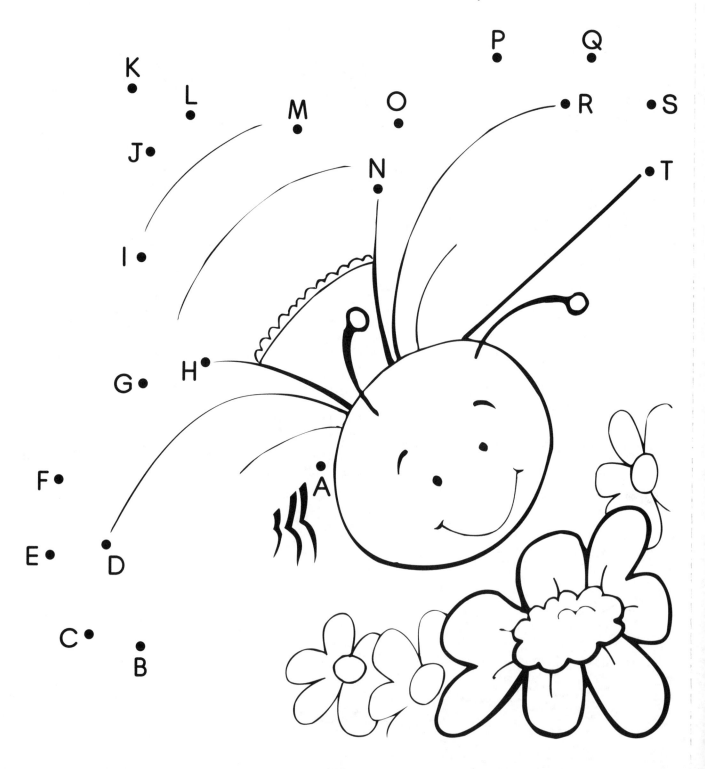

Essential Skills and Practice Grade PK

Let's Look Around

Connect the dots from **A** to **W**. Color the picture.

Snorkeling is a fun way to see ocean life.

Starfish

Connect the dots from **A** to **Z**. Color the picture.

I can grow new arms if I lose any.

Essential Skills and Practice Grade PK

Manatee

Connect the dots from **A** to **Z**. Color the picture.

I am sometimes called a sea cow.

I can eat 100 pounds of plants a day.

Name _____

Sea Lion

Connect the dots from **A** to **Z**. Color the picture.

I play and hunt in the ocean.

Essential Skills and Practice Grade PK

Desert Dweller

Connect the dots from **A** to **Z**. Color the picture.

Essential Skills and Practice Grade PK

Painting Pictures

Do you like to paint?

Connect the dots from **1** to **5**. Color the picture.

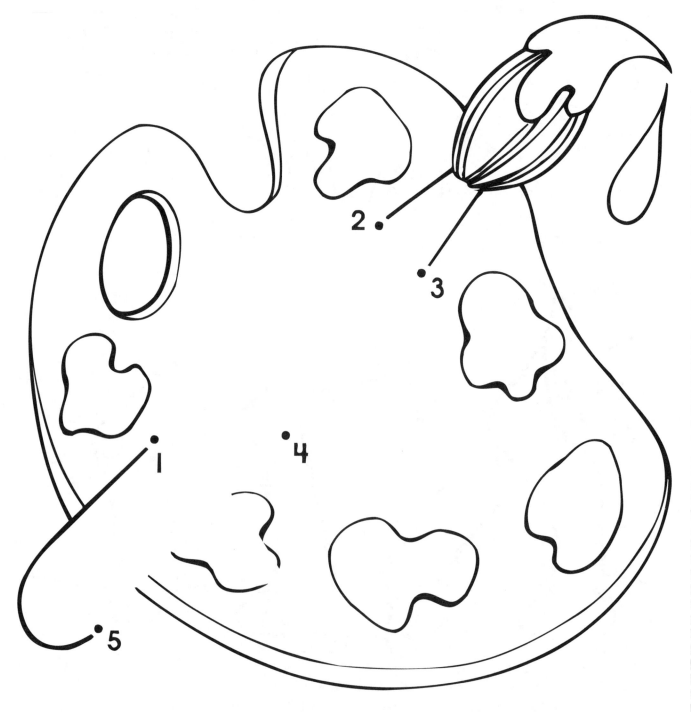

Mouse House

This is where Mitsy Mouse lives.

Connect the dots from **1** to **5**. Color the picture.

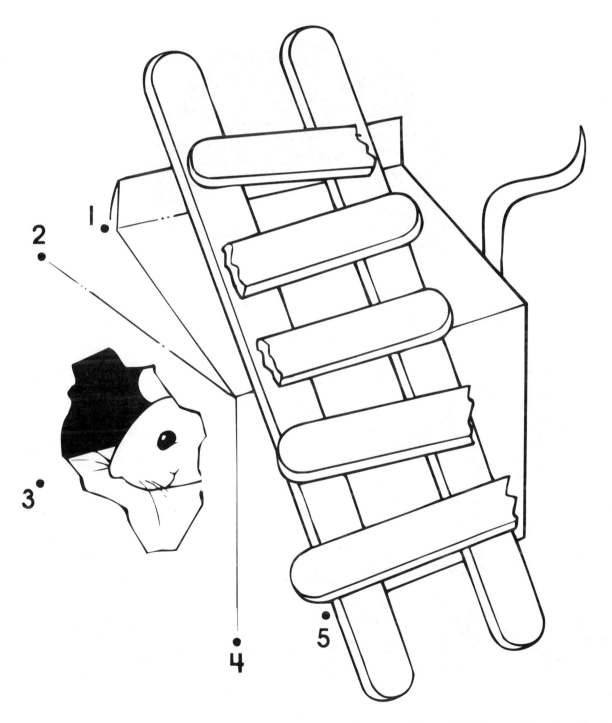

Essential Skills and Practice Grade PK

Delicious!

Joey loves sweet corn with butter!

Connect the dots from **1** to **5**. Color the picture.

Essential Skills and Practice Grade PK

Clam

Connect the dots from **1** to **5**. Color the picture.

I can dig with my special "foot."

Essential Skills and Practice Grade PK

Little Swimmer

This pet loves water.

Connect the dots from **1** to **10**. Color the picture.

Dress Up

It is fun to pretend. Who is Sarah dressed up like?

Connect the dots from **1** to **10**. Color the picture.

Essential Skills and Practice Grade PK

Up in the Sky

This is fun to play with on a windy day.

Connect the dots from **1** to **10**. Color the picture.

Essential Skills and Practice Grade PK

Marine Turtle

Connect the dots from **1** to **10**. Color the picture.

My flippers help me swim long distances.

Blue Whale

Connect the dots from **1** to **10**. Color the picture.

I am the largest animal in the world.

A Big Fisher

Pelicans live near the ocean to catch and eat fish.

Connect the dots from **1** to **15**. Color the picture.

Essential Skills and Practice Grade PK

Name _____

A Sweet Treat

This treat is fun to eat!

Connect the dots from **1** to **15**. Color the picture.

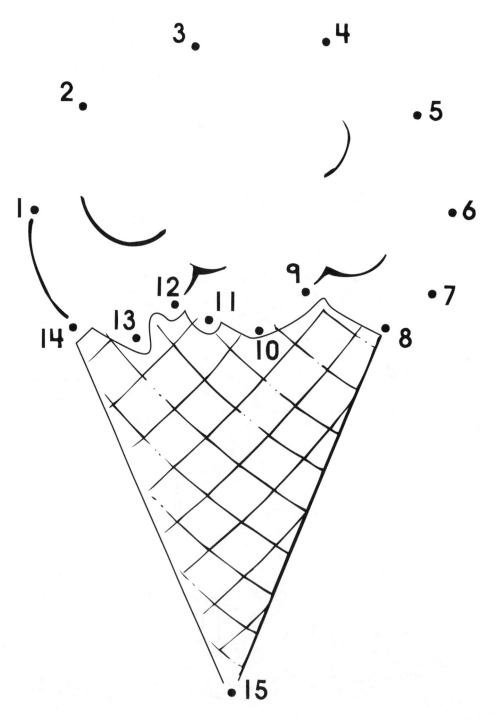

Essential Skills and Practice Grade PK

Let's Run

You might need these to run fast!

Connect the dots from **1** to **15**. Color the picture.

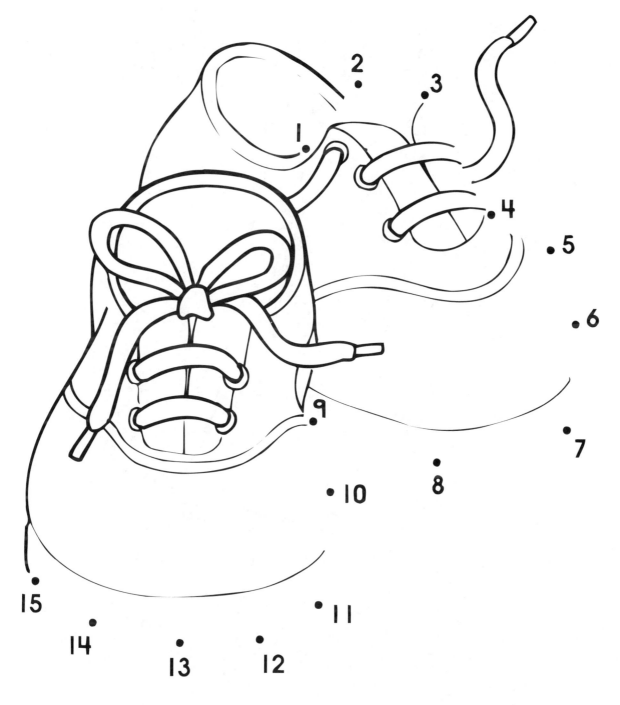

Essential Skills and Practice Grade PK

Cool on a Hot Day!

Nothing tastes sweeter on a hot day.

Connect the dots from **1** to **20**. Color the picture.

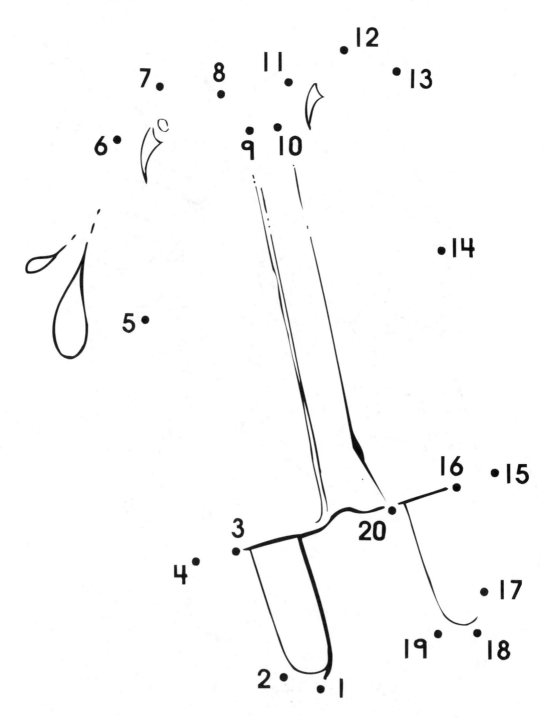

Essential Skills and Practice Grade PK

Let's Ride!

Monica loves to ride her horse, Spartan.

Connect the dots from **1** to **20**. Color the picture.

Essential Skills and Practice Grade PK

Cover Up

You will need this when it rains.

Connect the dots from **1** to **20**. Color the picture.

Name _____

Great in the Garden

This adds so much color to nature!

Connect the dots from **1** to **25**. Color the picture.

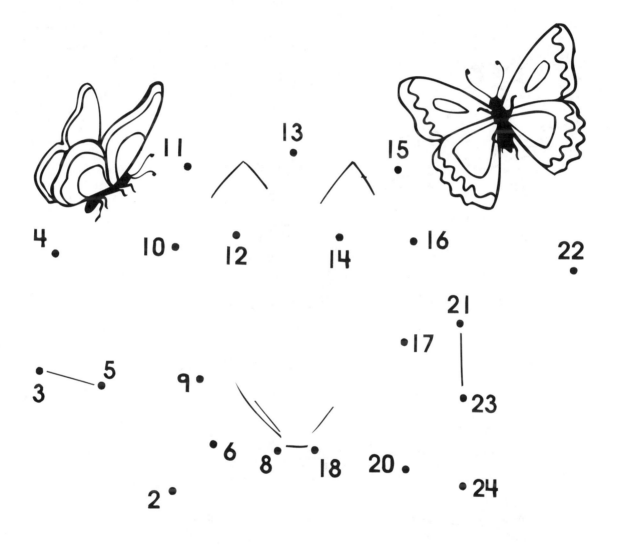

Essential Skills and Practice Grade PK

Name _____

Let's Go!

Kitty says, "Take me for a ride."

Connect the dots from **1** to **25**. Color the picture.

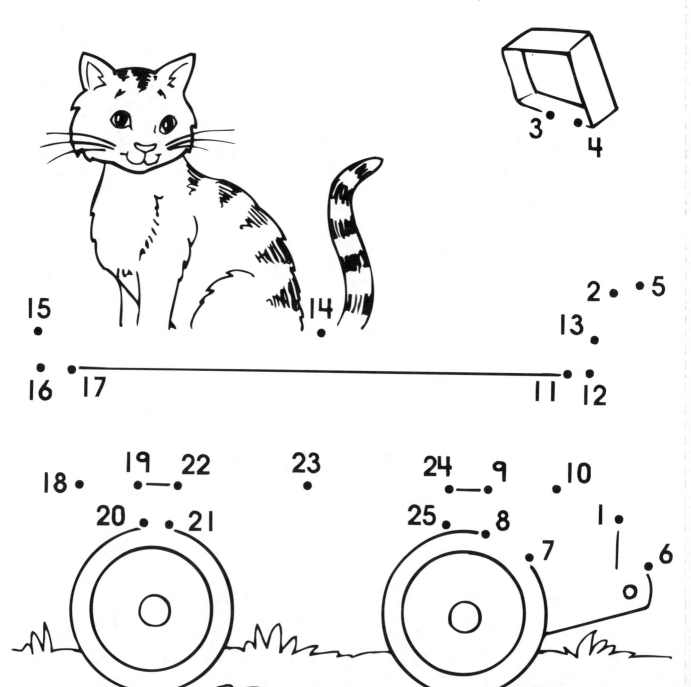

Essential Skills and Practice Grade PK

Flying Fish

Connect the dots from **1** to **25**. Color the picture.

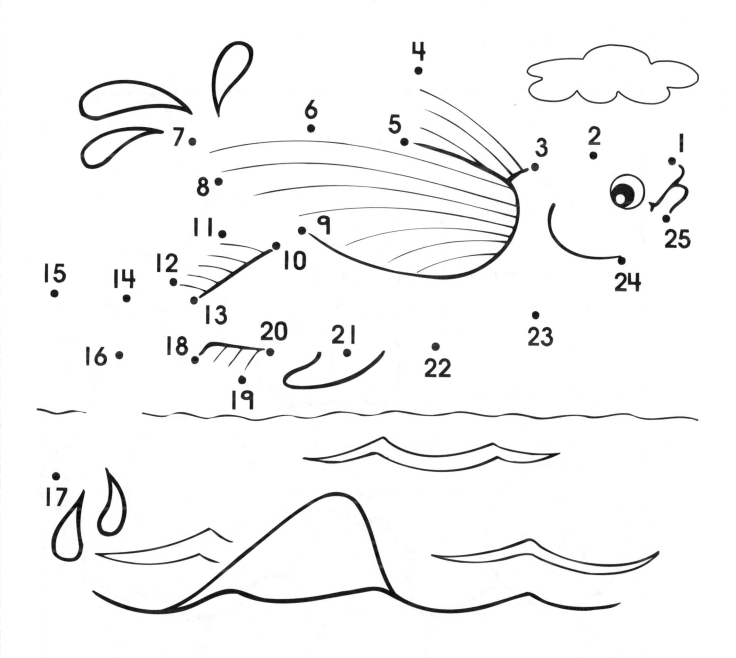

I can escape enemies by gliding through the air.

A Helpful Machine

You might see this on a farm.

Color the spaces with **b** red.

Color the spaces with **s** green.

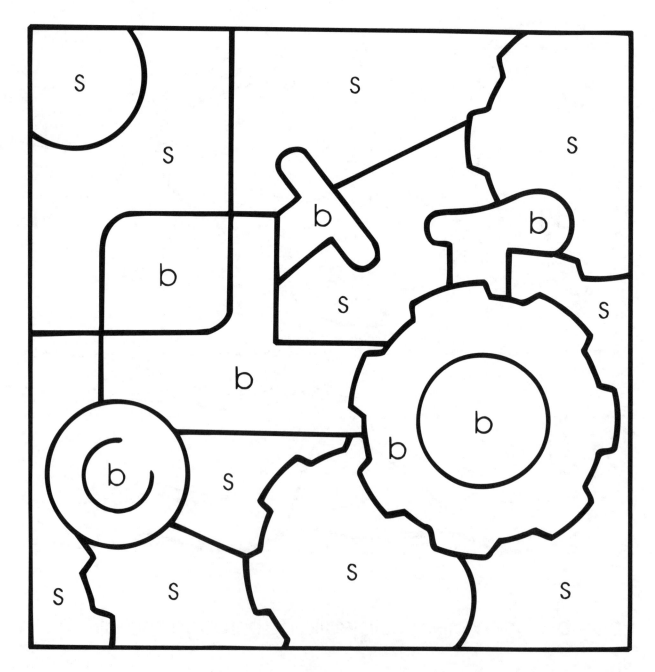

Hippity Hop

This animal has long, soft ears.

Color the spaces with **c** brown.

Color the spaces with **e** pink.

Essential Skills and Practice Grade PK

Name _____

Drip Drop

You need this on a rainy day.

Color the spaces with **d** orange.

Color the spaces with **w** blue.

264   Essential Skills and Practice Grade PK

So Very Tall

This animal has a very long neck.

Color the spaces with **h** brown.

Color the spaces with **f** orange.

Essential Skills and Practice Grade PK

Ding Dong

This is fun to ring!

Color the spaces with **s** purple.

Color the spaces with **z** yellow.

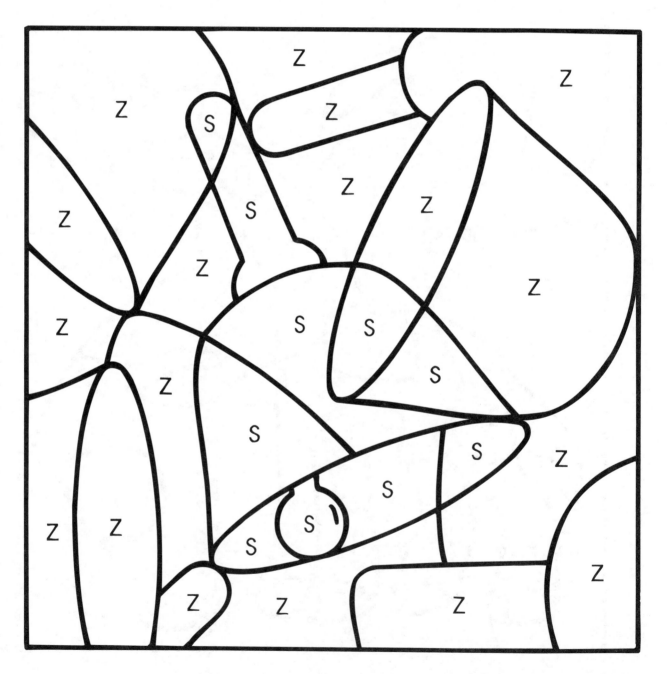

Essential Skills and Practice Grade PK

Go Out for a Pass!

This is fun to throw and catch!

Color the spaces with **t** brown.

Color the spaces with **q** green.

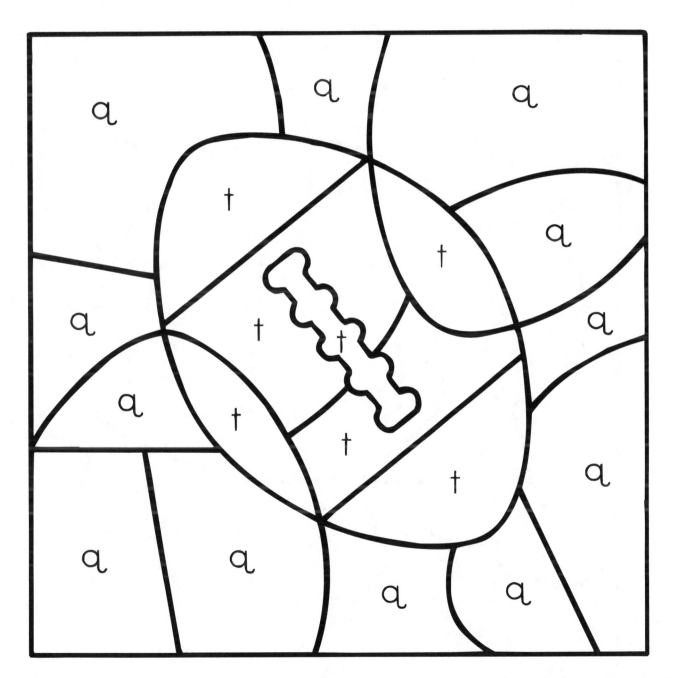

Home All the Time

This little animal carries its home on its back.

Color the spaces with **u** brown.

Color the spaces with **v** yellow.

Essential Skills and Practice Grade PK

Hop In

This can take you wherever you need to go.

Color the spaces with **x** blue.

Color the spaces with **i** green.

269   *Essential Skills and Practice Grade PK*

A Super Trunk

This animal has a very long trunk.

Color the spaces with **A** red.

Color the spaces with **W** gray.

Essential Skills and Practice Grade PK

Fly, Fly Away

This beautiful creature can be seen around flowers.

Color the spaces with **A** orange.

Color the spaces with **F** yellow.

Color the spaces with **H** green.

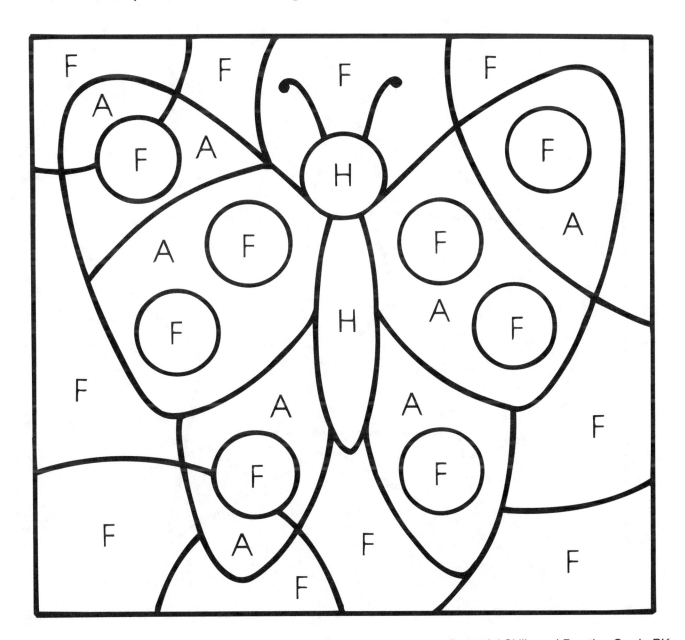

Twinkle, Twinkle

You can see this in the sky at night.

Color the spaces with **B** yellow.

Color the spaces with **H** blue.

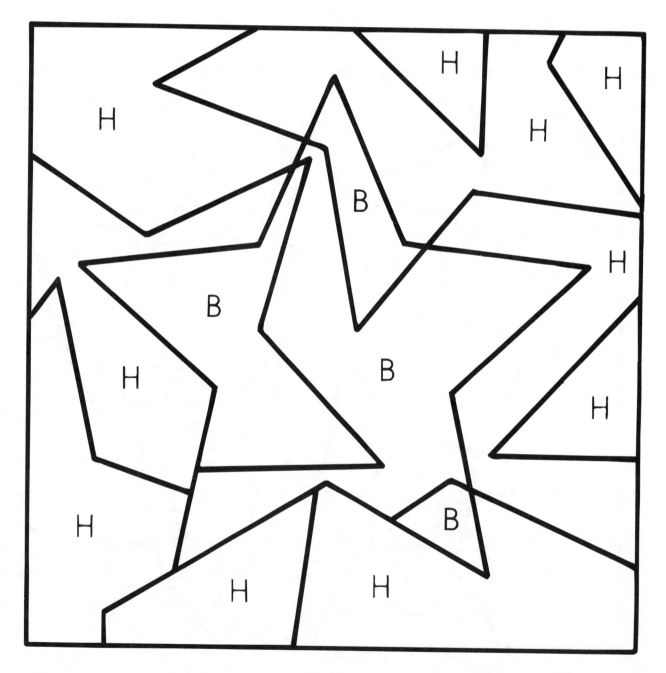

Dig Deep

This truck can dig deep holes.

Color the spaces with **B** yellow.

Color the spaces with **P** black.

Color the spaces with **W** orange.

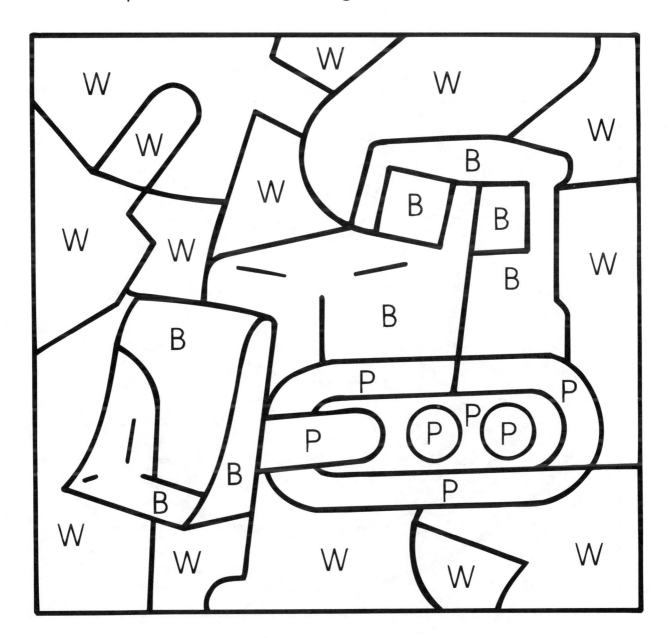

273

Let's Rock

You rock back and forth when you ride me.

Color the spaces with **C** blue.

Color the spaces with **V** purple.

Color the spaces with **Q** pink.

Super Swimmer

This animal lives in the water.

Color the spaces with **D** blue.

Color the spaces with **N** orange.

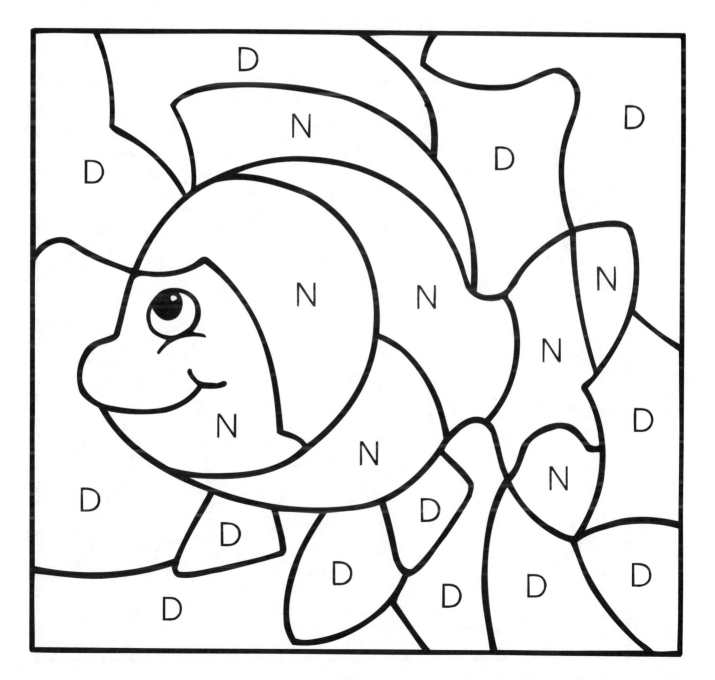

Essential Skills and Practice Grade PK

Cool and Sweet

What a cool summertime treat!

Color the spaces with **D** pink.

Color the spaces with **O** brown.

Color the spaces with **U** yellow.

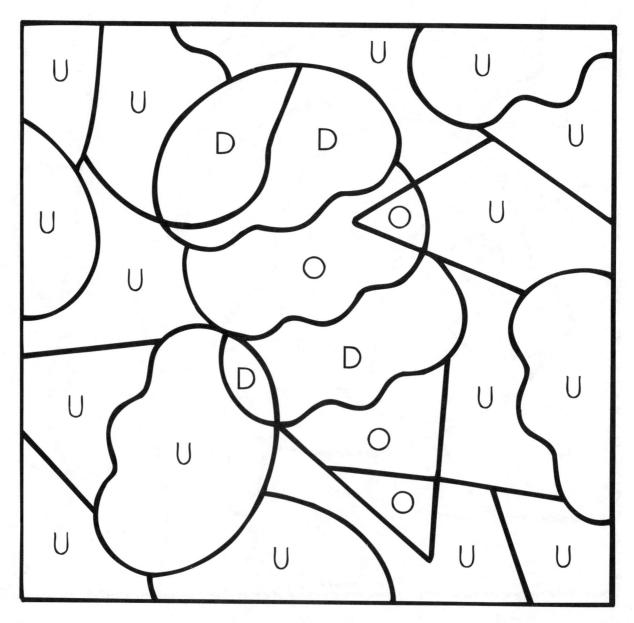

Essential Skills and Practice Grade PK

Lots of Color

This blooms in spring.

Color the spaces with **E** green.

Color the spaces with **H** pink.

Color the spaces with **T** yellow.

Yum!

What a sweet treat!

Color the spaces with **F** pink.

Color the spaces with **K** yellow.

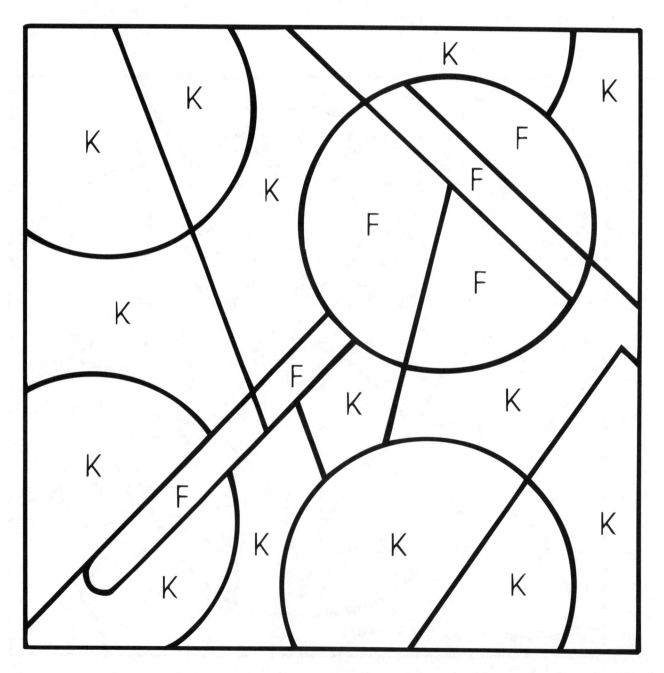

Essential Skills and Practice Grade PK

Sweet and Juicy

This crunchy fruit is a tasty treat.

Color the spaces with **G** red.

Color the spaces with **V** blue.

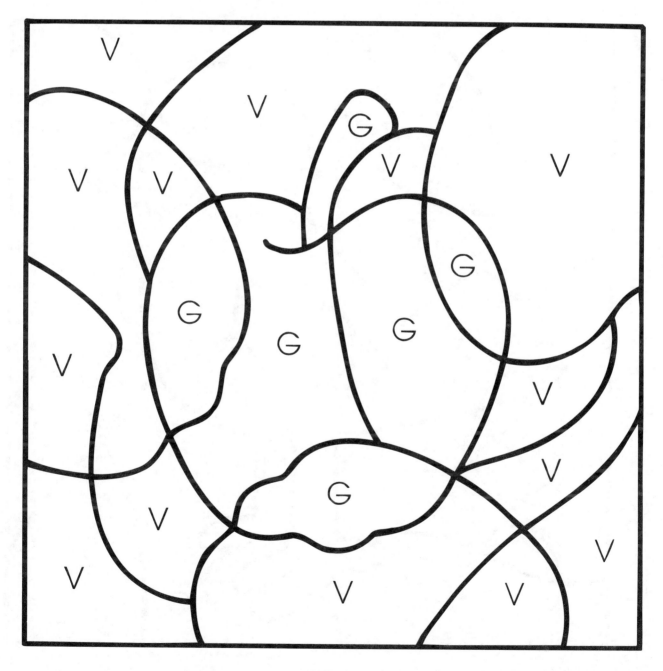

Essential Skills and Practice Grade PK

Wonderful Wings

This animal's wings help it fly up in the sky.

Color the spaces with **M** pink.

Color the spaces with **C** blue.

Party Time

You might see these at a party.

Color the spaces with **O** green.

Color the spaces with **X** blue.

Color the spaces with **S** pink.

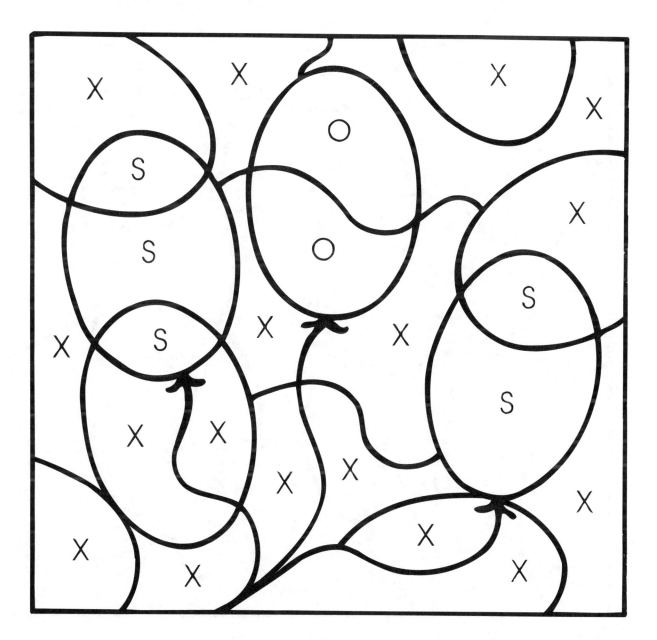

Oink! Oink!

This animal loves to play in the mud.

Color the spaces with **R** pink.

Color the spaces with **T** orange.

Essential Skills and Practice Grade PK

Clowning Around

He makes people laugh and smile.

Color to find the hidden picture.

● = red   ● ● = yellow   ● ● ● = blue

Essential Skills and Practice Grade PK

Black and White

This striped animal can be found at the zoo.

Color to find the hidden picture.

⠿ = white   ⠿ = red

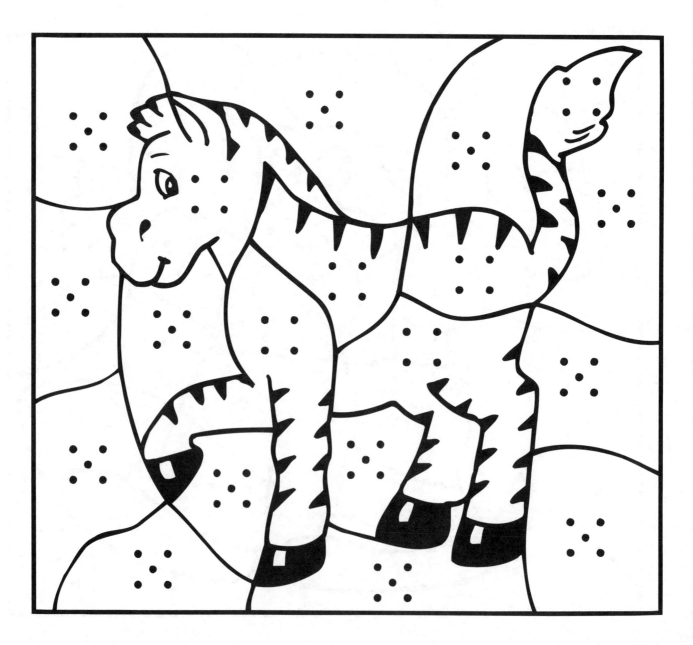

Sky High

This is fun to fly on a windy day.

Color to find the hidden picture.

= orange   = purple   = blue

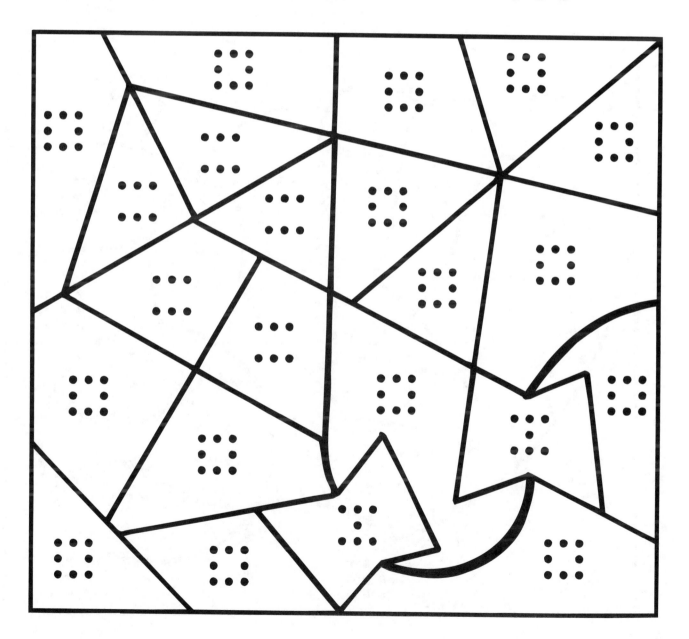

Essential Skills and Practice Grade PK

Batter Up!

These things are used in a summer sport.

Color to find the hidden picture.

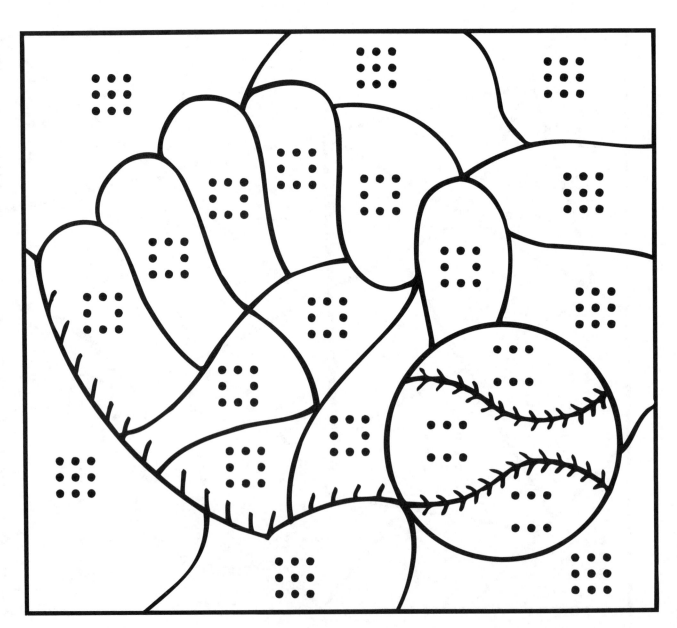

Essential Skills and Practice Grade PK

Quack! Quack!

This animal quacks and lives near ponds.

Color to find the hidden picture.

= yellow   = blue   = orange

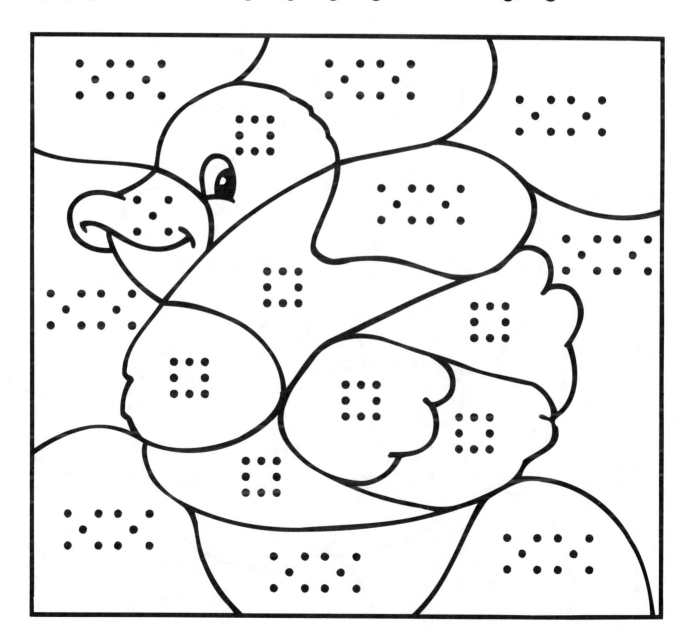

Flipper

This playful animal lives in the ocean.

Color to find the hidden picture.

Name _____

Can This Dragon Fly?

This insect likes to fly near water.

Color to find the hidden picture.

1 = green   **2** = blue   **3** = yellow

Essential Skills and Practice Grade PK

Strum and Hum

You can make beautiful music with this.

Color to find the hidden picture.

3 = brown   **4** = orange   **5** = yellow

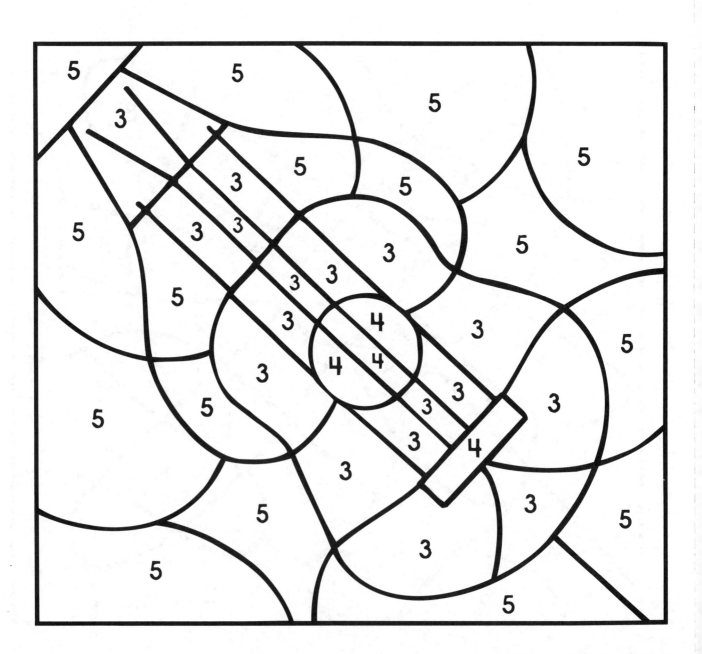

Essential Skills and Practice Grade PK

Polly Want a Cracker?

You might hear this animal talk!

Color to find the hidden picture.

2 = red   **4** = yellow   **6** = blue   **8** = green

I Can Change!

This little animal can turn into a beautiful butterfly!

Color to find the hidden picture.

3 = brown   **7** = black   **8** = blue   **9** = green

Leaping Lizards!

This reptile has a scaly body.

Color to find the hidden picture.

7 = green   **8** = brown   **9** = black   **10** = yellow

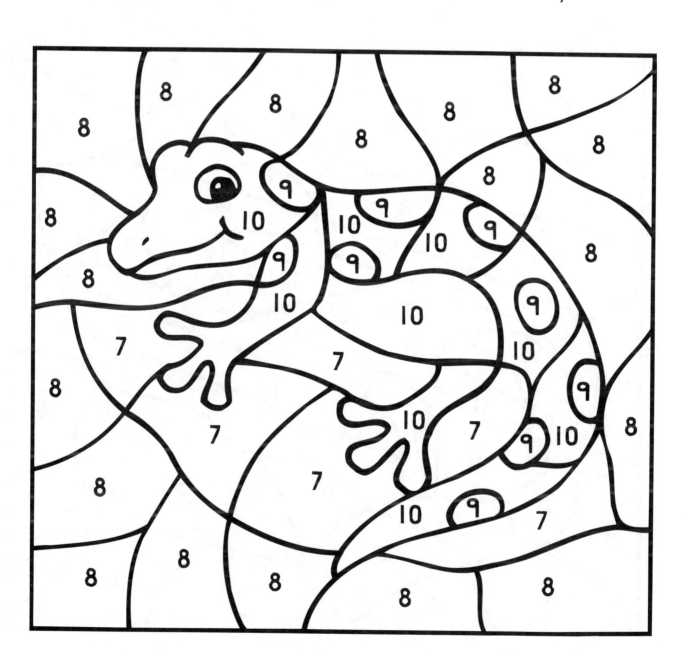

Cruising Along

This can bounce or jump over waves.

Color to find the hidden picture.

8 = blue   **9** = red   **10** = black

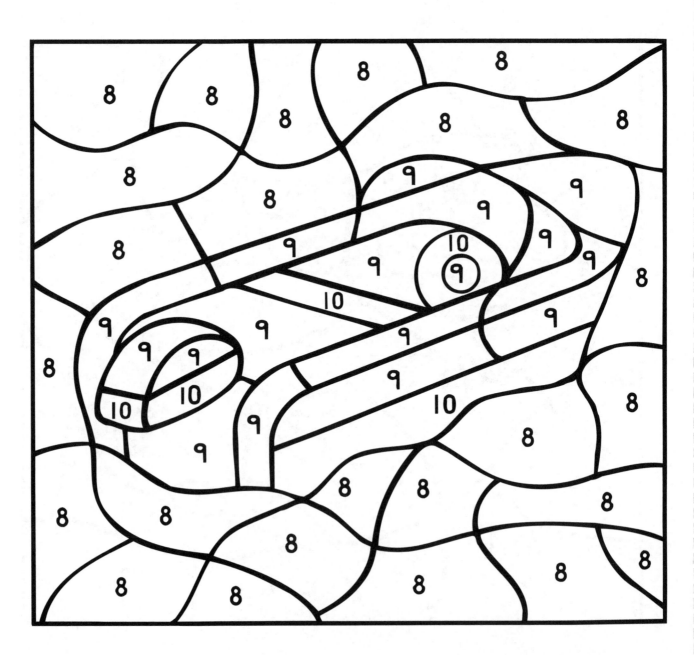

Essential Skills and Practice Grade PK

Butterflies

Color a path to the flowers.

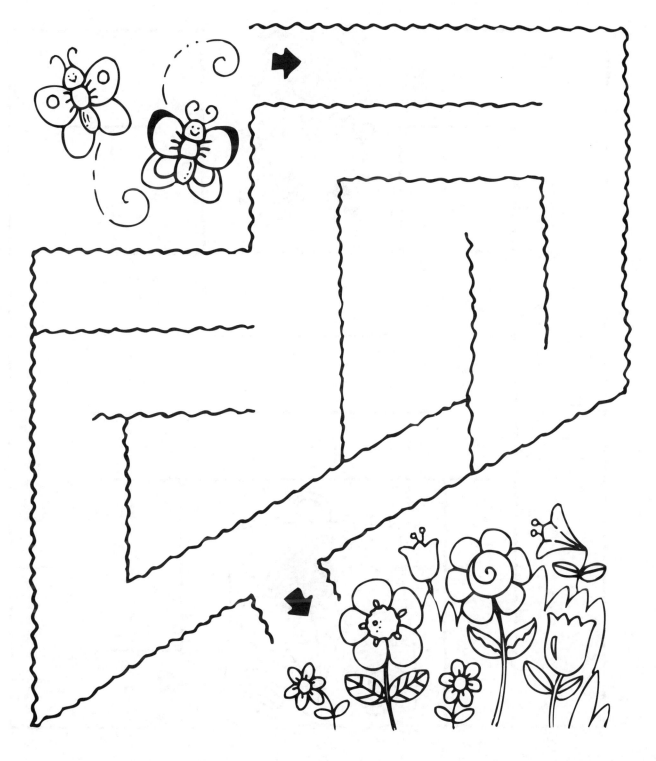

Essential Skills and Practice Grade PK

It's in the Bag

Put the bear in the bag.

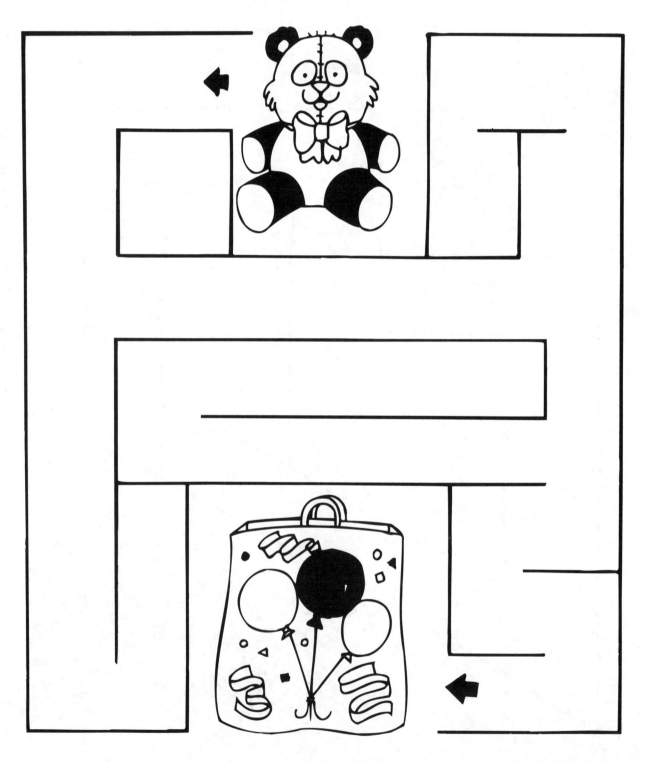

Scarecrows

Help the scarecrow find her friend.

Essential Skills and Practice Grade PK

The Chick

Help the chick through the egg.

The Tree

Lead the family to the tree.

Essential Skills and Practice Grade PK

Time to Eat

Color a path from the bread to the boy.

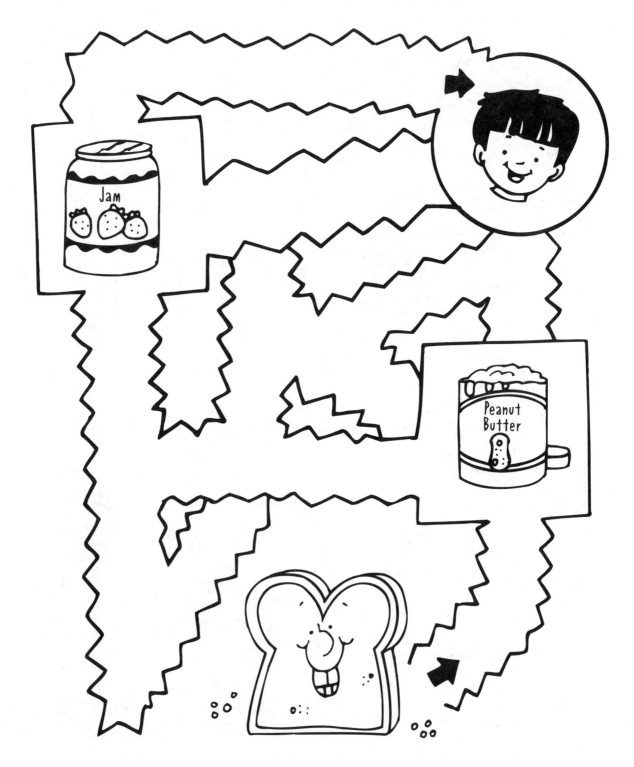

Essential Skills and Practice Grade PK

Tea Time

Fill the cups with tea.

Essential Skills and Practice Grade PK

Popcorn Party

Color a path to the bowl of popcorn.

Essential Skills and Practice Grade PK

Camping

Color a path to the camp.

Essential Skills and Practice Grade PK

Missing Treats

Find the candy.

Let's Sing

Color a path to the music.

Essential Skills and Practice Grade PK

Pyramids

Lead the camel to the pyramids.

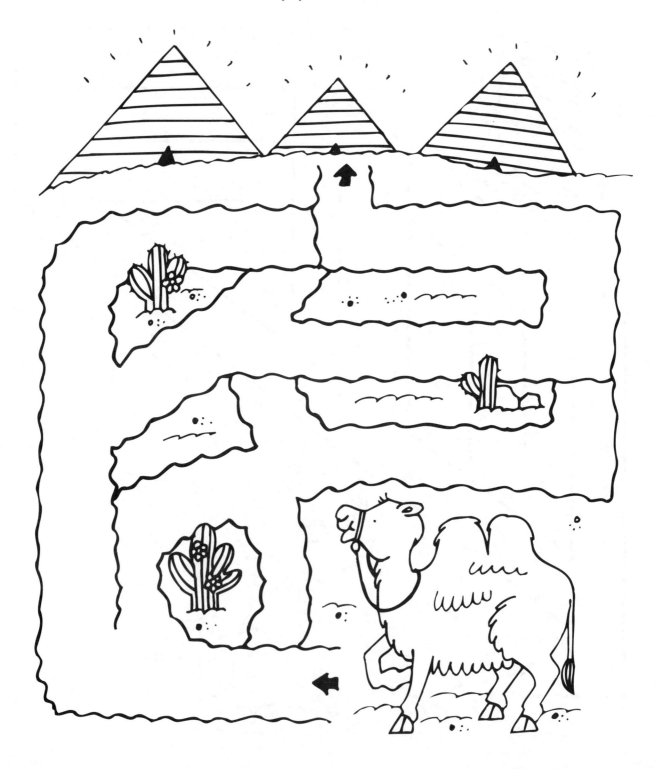

Essential Skills and Practice Grade PK

Lion Tamer

Color a path to the lion.

Essential Skills and Practice Grade PK

Hot Soup

Color a path to the pot of soup.

Essential Skills and Practice Grade PK

Lizard Fun

Help the lizard to the stump.

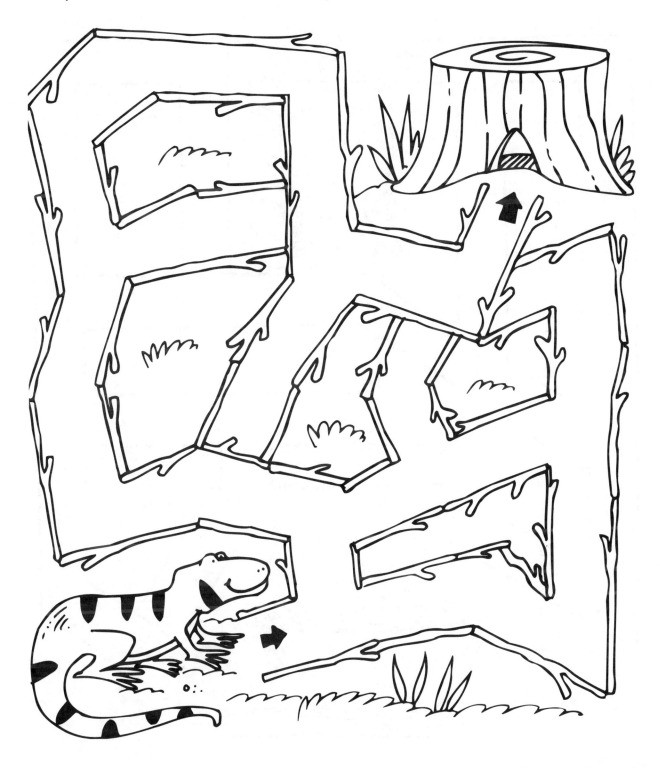

Essential Skills and Practice Grade PK

Breakfast Time

Color a path to the bowl.

Essential Skills and Practice Grade PK

Fun at the Park

Color the path to the bottom of the ride.

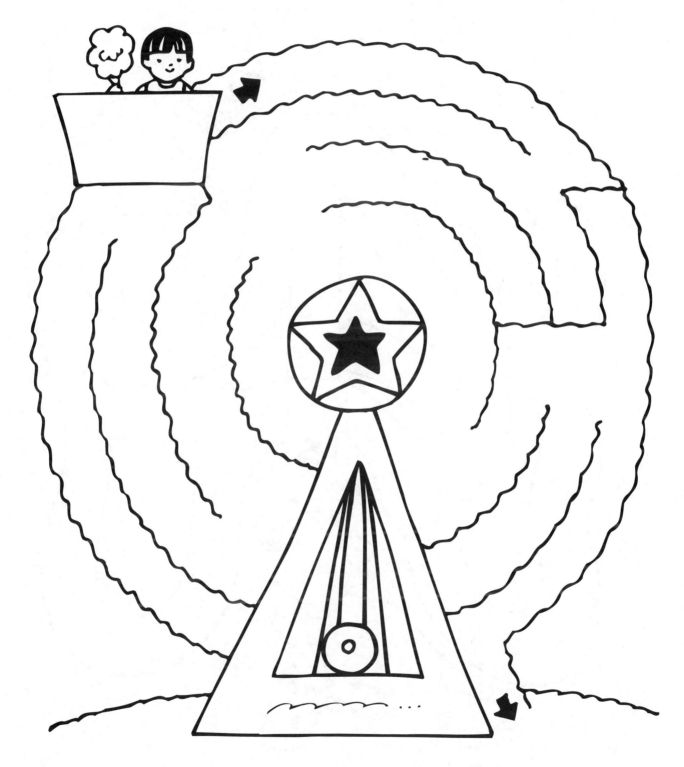

Dinosaur Friends

Help the dinosaur find his friends.

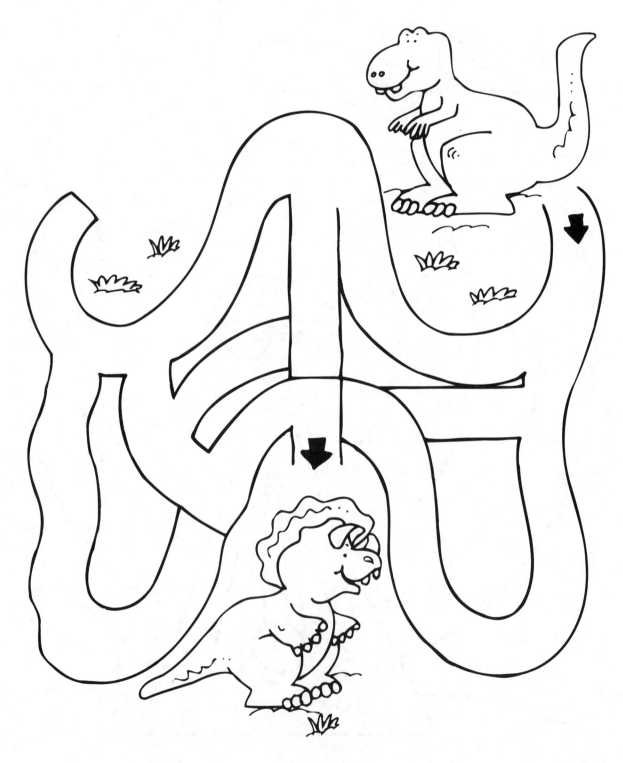

Essential Skills and Practice Grade PK

Name _____

Ice Cream

Color a path to the ice cream.

Essential Skills and Practice Grade PK

A Hole in One

Hit the ball into the hole.

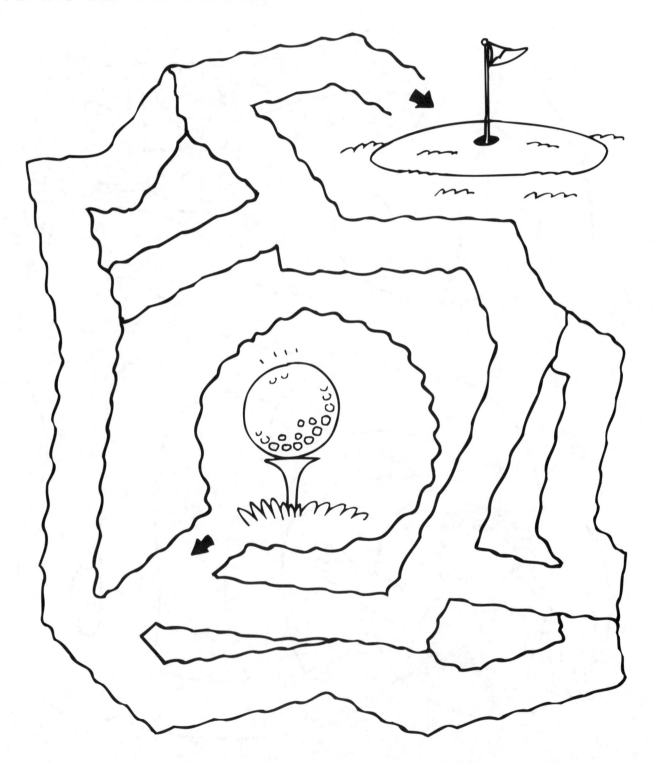

Essential Skills and Practice Grade PK

Cookies

Color a path to the cookies.

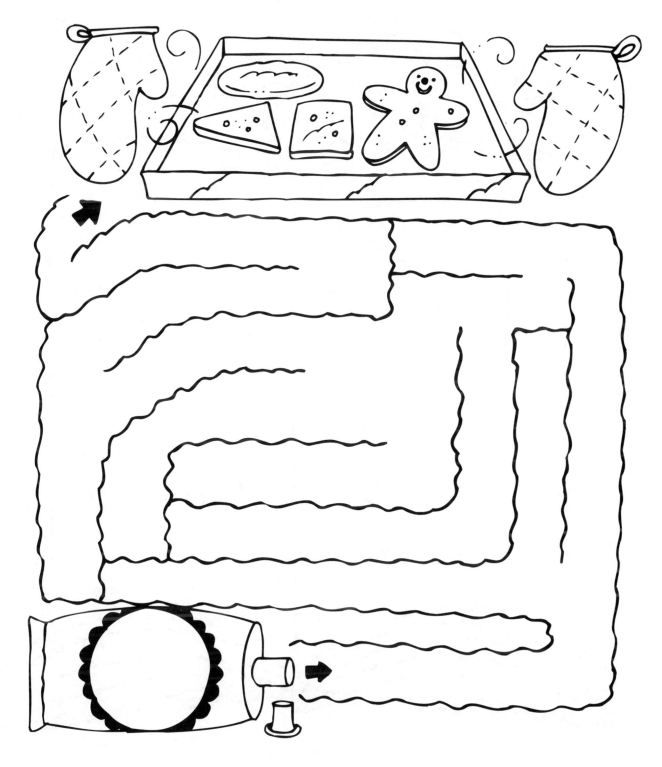

Essential Skills and Practice Grade PK

The Bookworm

Color a path through the book.

Apple Snack

Color a path to the apple.

Essential Skills and Practice Grade PK

Lost and Found

Find the lost puppy.

Over the Net

Get the ball over the net.

Essential Skills and Practice Grade PK

Score!

Color a path to the goal.

Essential Skills and Practice Grade PK